ESSENTIAL BELIEVING
FOR THE CHRISTIAN SOUL

*

Believe in everything
important in life

Michael Joachim Girard

To the Brunette Family,
Best Wishes!

Mike Girard

xulon PRESS

I dedicate this book to my daughters, Christina and Alexandra. In the spirit of the story *The Polar Express*, may you always have the courage and will to believe, hearing truth, good, love, and God along the journey of life. Live your ideals, dream your dreams, hold your most cherished hopes, and in the face of opposition and difficulty, let faith be your inspiration, guide, and strength. I love you always.

I extend to my parents, William and Doris, deep heartfelt gratitude for all they have done for me. All their love and the family they created have made this work of the head and heart possible. I thank my brother Tom and sisters Regina, Angela, Pauline, and Theresa for their part of the fertile ground of family and relationships in which faith is planted, takes root, grows, blossoms forth, and is fruitful. Thank you.

I acknowledge my former philosophy professors, Donald Demarco, Rev. Clair Girodat, Gerard Campbell and Floyd Centore, from St. Jerome's College at the University of Waterloo, Ontario. Your beliefs and love of truth have shaped my mind and instilled in me a profound love and respect for truth. In memory and gratitude.

To all my students past, present, and future – may you see your questions reflected in the words and answers I offer. Thank you for your wonder and your questions. Keep thinking and always believe.

I also wish to thank all those who helped in any way in bringing this work to completion. I thank my proof-readers: My sister Angela Zurkirchen, Megan Murphy, Cheryl Graham, Nancy O'Donnell, and most importantly, Erin Hilderley. I thank Sylvia Burleigh and Iyse Lee at Xulon Press for their reassuring professionalism and patience.

I sincerely acknowledge the entire Christian community of believers past and present, and all those who have instructed me in the Christian faith. I acknowledge my parents who, by word and example, were my first teachers of the faith. Above all, I acknowledge Jesus Christ, the Incarnate Word, whose ideals, values, principles, teachings, and truths I have tried to accurately convey.

Contents

~ Greater and Beyond ~

~ Human Beings ~

~ Things Human ~

~ Relationship ~

~ Important Things ~

~ Basic Things ~

~ Transcendent Things ~

~ Life of the Spirit ~

~ God and Angels ~

~ Things of God ~

~ Spiritual Things ~

~ Additional Important Things ~

~ Special Addition ~

Preface

Ever since I can remember, I've had a desire to write a book and I knew someday I would. This is that book and little did I know my two children would be the occasion and catalyst for it. On January 2, 2005, my daughters Christina and Alexandra and I went to see the movie *The Polar Express*. This event set everything in motion. Soon after seeing the film, I began writing down the many different things that came to mind that I thought were important to believe in. They were conjoined with the words "even when" or "even though," as I sensed we all need encouragement and motivation to believe. That was followed by a grouping of the different lines into common themes, and this eventuated into verses of four, five or six lines. Later, the verses developed into sets of five stanzas. For some reason, a set of five stanzas on the same theme worked very well, in terms of having ample space to express the idea and get the point across succinctly without making it too brief.

At times, it seemed like it wasn't I doing the writing. I liken the experience to traveling down the river in a canoe. I am paddling and steering but the main force and reason for my movement is the current of the river beneath me. All I have to do is steer in the right direction until I arrive at my destination. I can even close my eyes and do nothing, yet I still move along. I have felt and sensed that God has been the current beneath me during this work and I would like to acknowledge this fact.

I make no claim in stating any new or original ideas, for the matter and content of my writing are the basic undercurrents of life and living, realist philosophy in the tradition of Aristotle and St. Thomas Aquinas, and basic Christian teachings. As such, they are all the common lot of mankind. My contribution is my unique form and way of expressing the ideas and content, of which I am blessed to possess. My experience as a teacher helps me explain and present concepts in a straightforward and understandable fashion.

I sincerely hope that my intention to share essential things to believe for the believing and practicing Christian will prove to be both enlightening and fruitful. I believe there is a quiet Christian reawakening and resurgence happening in the world today. With this in mind, I offer *Essential Believing For The Christian Soul* with two basic intentions. My first intention is that this book will be a strong reminder and wakeup call that it is indeed most important and essential *that we believe*. My second intention is to offer people in written form important and essential content of *what to believe*. Let us confirm each other in our common faith, and pray for one another, as we journey together to the one, true, and living God of us all. All to the greater glory of God.

Prologue

It was New Year's Day and the Christmas season was soon ending. On the short list of things to do before the end of the holidays was going to a movie together, a family tradition at Christmas time. The girls suggested *The Polar Express*. I told them that I usually don't view animated films and I wasn't excited about going to see this particular one. They said it was the Christmas movie of the season and tomorrow would be the last chance to keep our tradition going. It was an easy sell and I obliged.

The next day, we joined the throng of people at the mall, like us, taking advantage of the opportunities of the final day of the holiday season. At the cinema, I got into the ticket line while the girls went to the concession to get some refreshments. Alexandra said, "Dad, don't say Polar Bear Express – it's Polar Express." She knew me well and knew I was prone to utter things, such as that, consciously or unconsciously. When I got to the ticket person, I said, "Three for the Polar Bear Express!" I could afford the banter, as my girls were not beside me to be embarrassed by my antics. I wasn't anticipating a great movie, but at least I was open to enjoying the occasion with my two daughters and making it a special time.

We were early and enjoyed frozen yogurt as we awaited the lights to dim and the movie to start. When it began, I was immediately surprised and impressed by the high quality of the animation. I had never seen anything like it before. As the story unfolded, I began to enjoy it. It was turning out to be a very good story about a boy who was not sure if he believed in Santa Claus, and his amazing journey to the North Pole in a mysterious train. I wasn't surprised when the boy was chosen by Santa to receive the first gift of Christmas. The gift was a beautiful jingle bell and he told the boy it was a symbol of the spirit of Christmas, as is Santa himself. Santa Claus continued by telling the boy not to forget that the true spirit of Christmas lies within one's heart. It was an unforgettable moment when the boy whispered, "I believe," and then heard the sound of the bell. Before that moment, the bell was silent and made no sound. His act of believing enabled him to hear the bell and the sound indicated and confirmed to the boy, that Santa Claus was indeed real and true. The boy was happy and his doubts put to rest.

I think Santa wanted to teach the boy something else, something deeper. He told the boy that both the bell and Santa Claus are symbols of the Christmas spirit. Santa is not the greatest thing about Christmas, even though he is a grand figure in the hearts and imaginations of us all. The greatest thing about Christmas is the Christmas spirit - the spirit of love, joy, peace, hope, wonder, forgiveness, giving, generosity, and all that is good. The boy is old enough to begin to understand, moving from the material things of Christmas to a deeper meaning, namely the spirit of Christmas. I think Santa wanted the boy to believe in the spirit of Christmas, and in so doing, the boy will experience in the years to come, that wonderful spirit, bringing it to life, just as he brought the sound of the bell to life.

On Christmas Day, the boy's parents did not hear the sound of the bell, but the boy and his sister heard it. The boy and his sister believed in Santa Claus and the Christmas spirit embodied in him. The parents, apparently, did not believe, neither in Santa Claus nor in the spirit of Christmas. They did not believe, and they did not hear.

I left the theater with a deep sense of satisfaction and a smile on my face. I was glad the girls picked *The Polar Express* to see and it was truly a memorable and special time with them. Although they are twenty and sixteen years old, we enjoy these kinds of family activities together very much.

As busy and preoccupied as I was, with starting back to work, in the back of my mind was the movie and the words, "If you believe, you will hear the bell." Other words echoed in my mind – "Believe and you will see. Believe and you will know. Believe and you will understand. Believe and you will experience. Believe and you will…" Yes, believing is so important and it opens the door to so many things in life and living.

Christina was leaving the next day, and I thought giving the girls a bell would be a nice little symbolic gift to end the holiday season with. After work on Monday, I spent two hours looking around for Christmas bells. I noticed little Christmas stockings at a department store, which I thought would be perfect. I ended up buying two little Christmas stockings with "From Santa" on them, and two small bells from a craft store. The stockings were perfect because they were clearly from Santa, just like the gift box in the movie. That night I placed the bells in the stockings and carefully wrapped them. I selected two extra special Christmas tags, wrote their names on them, and added, "The first gift of Christmas – from Santa."

I gave Christina her gift on the way to the airport early the next morning and she opened it on the plane. I was busy all evening and didn't get a chance to get in contact with her until late at night. I sent her an email: "Hi Christina, glad you got back to London, okay. I'm sure you're asleep right now. I just got back from curling - we had the late game tonight so it's been a very long day for me. Canada won the World Junior Hockey Championship – that's great! Remember, if you believe, you will hear the bell. Take care, love Dad."

Even though it was very late by now, Christina emailed me back: "Dad, thank you so much for the gift! It took me a second to figure out the meaning of the bell but then I realized it was from the movie! What a nice little gift... I hung the stocking and bell on a hook in my room so it can remind me of you and how important it is to believe in not only the Christmas spirit but anything in life that is important. I had a great time on the holidays, watching Lord of the Rings and doing the puzzle. It really was a nice Christmas! Thanks again, Christina."

Her quick response was indeed a very nice surprise, surpassed by the fact that she readily acknowledged that it is important to believe in things that are important in life. That was my unwritten intention when I wrapped the bell and the stocking, and I hoped we could talk about it some time later. As a parent, hearing that from my twenty-year-old daughter was an extra special Christmas gift for me!

Introduction

I believe humanity is now at one of the most critical cross-roads in human history. In the continual march of development and the relentless drive for progress, we continue to push the boundaries and limits of knowledge and technology. Never before thought of possibilities in human genetics are now realities today. The Internet has literally taken facts, information, and knowledge to a new level, and all at the stroke of a key, in split second time. However, do we understand more and are we any wiser? Are we better people? Are we truly any happier? Are we making real progress? Is the world a better place?

As I look around, I see societies and the world at large in great disarray. Our fragile planet is in very rough shape, in need of betterment and positive change. Wars, fighting, crime, and pollution are ravaging our world. People appear to be very confused and alienated. Relationships today are not as lasting and permanent as they were a generation ago. We live in a fractured and broken world. Love of God and neighbor has been replaced with love of self. Discipline and morality are not given priority and importance as they should. Death and destruction pervade our world, and life is not valued and respected as God meant it to be. Things of the spirit have given way to materialism and hedonism. We have lost the sense of truth in the intellectual realm and lost touch with objective good and right in the moral order. We have literally turned our backs on God as a people and nation. We do not acknowledge, follow, and worship God as we ought. People, individually and collectively, have chosen the path of materialism and self-centered selfishness, where man is the measure of all things.

Despite all the great negative aspects, there always remains the possibility of a better, safer, and happier world for us all. There is always hope because there is always God. There is hope because humans are fundamentally good in their nature and everyone has the potential for good. Nevertheless, we need to regain or forge anew a healthy frame of reference, one grounded and always connected to reality and to the real and authentic lived experiences of humankind. We need truth and the objective good. We need love and real hope for a better world. We need faith and connection to the true and living God. We need to live our faith and put it into practice and action despite the many difficulties and obstacles we encounter. We need to believe that a better world is both possible and attainable.

Believing is the simple, common, and practical way for people to make the important connections in life. Believing in God's revelation enables us to attain knowledge of certain truths we would not otherwise possess. Not only is believing essential for us as humans, we are hardwired to believe and it is natural to believe. *That* we believe is one thing and *what* we believe is another. Hence, I share with you the reader, things I believe and hold to be true and things I believe and hold to be good.

The over one hundred and fifty diverse topics cover six basic themes, namely truth, love, faith, hope, good, and most importantly, God. There are other related themes such as life, happiness, fulfillment, relationship, striving, achievement, purpose, meaning and transcendence. I believe these are the main ingredients in the recipe for personal transformation, societal change, betterment and peace in the world. I believe these basic themes are the ingredients in the tonic for individual and collective happiness and fulfillment. I think these themes are the elements which, in the degree we possess and live them, will determine our future and destiny.

Believing can be understood in two basic and distinct ways. One is believing something and the other is believing *in* something. The first is believing or holding a statement, proposition, or assertion to be true, as in, "I believe there are angels in heaven." The second is believing in something or holding something to be good, wonderful, useful, beautiful, beneficial, etc. We see, acknowledge, and attribute some basic value to that which we believe in. For example, "I believe in friendship," meaning I believe in the value of friendship and all the good there is with it. When we believe, we also to some degree, invest, devote, and commit ourselves to what we believe in. Thus, we can believe in the truth of things as well as in the value and goodness of things.

Believing in everything important in life is at once both human and necessary. It is at the essence of what it means to be a human being and what life is all about. Believing is personal. Our beliefs are ours; nobody can believe for us. Our beliefs and what we believe in, reveal who we really are at a heart and soul level. This "believing in" is open, rich, fertile, and encompasses so much in life. Believing and the beliefs we hold humanize us; it gives us meaning; it gives us something to strive for; it gives us hope and optimism; it gives us purpose; it grounds us; it guides and directs us; it connects us; it engages and commits us; it gives us what we need; it is necessary for happiness. Believing helps us to transcend ourselves and actualize our potential. Believing connects us to what is good, true, and beautiful in life, and allows us to live lives of faith, hope, and love. Believing brings us face to face with the mystery of God. Believing is one of the keys to life and happiness. Believing is absolutely essential.

I offer my views, not as one opinion among all others, but humbly and openly as "kernels of truth on the cob of life," as food and sustenance for our wanting spirits and hungry souls. I personally believe and hold all that I have written and as I recall the poignant words of John Henry Cardinal Newman, "Cor ad cor loquitur" – "Heart speaks to heart," I invite you to read and take my words to heart. Although I have a background in philosophy and I am a teacher by profession, I speak in common language to all people. I am not a theologian or official teacher of any Christian church, and as such, I do not claim or speak with any authority of my own. God *is* the authority and I am simply a sincere believer trying to be faithful. Hence, the judgment of the truth of the words you are about to read, I reserve to God, who *is* Truth and to you, the reader into whose mind and heart truth enters slowly and gently, only to gain strength and authority by its own accord and character. May God bless you.

"Believe in everything important in life... For purpose and meaning, happiness and fulfillment, life and destiny depend upon it."

~ Author

~ Encouragement ~

Stepping Out in Faith

Believe in risk –
sometimes we are called to venture forth.

Believe in adventure –
there is more to life than the straight path.

Believe in taking a chance –
you will never know until you try.

Believe in openness –
be open to whatever opportunities come your way.

Believe in stepping out in faith –
move forward even though you can't see the end.

~ Believe

Better Times

Believe in optimism –
pessimism will get you nowhere.

Believe in being positive –
being negative will only weigh you down.

Believe in better times and days –
have patience and perseverance.

Believe in the future –
there are many opportunities for good.

Believe in a better world –
for you, for me and for everybody.

~ Believe

Don't Give Up

Believe in trying something,
even when you've never done it before.

Believe in getting back up,
even when you have taken a heavy fall.

Believe in learning,
even when you are having difficulty.

Believe in accomplishment,
even when you have yet to attain it.

Believe in not giving up,
even when you are very tired and weary.

~ Believe

Overcoming Difficulty

Believe in facing,
the greatest fear paralyzing you.

Believe in meeting,
the greatest challenge of your life.

Believe in conquering,
the greatest obstacle in your way.

Believe in resolving,
the greatest problem before you.

Believe in overcoming,
the greatest difficulty you experience.

~ Believe

Optimism and Hope

Believe in better days ahead,
even when all seems hopeless.

Believe in an end to the pain,
even when the suffering is constant.

Believe in a relief to the burden,
even when the struggle seems endless.

Believe in a resolution to the problem,
even when there doesn't appear to be an answer.

Believe in optimism and hope,
even when things are dark and gloomy.

~ Believe

Words into Action

Believe in putting words into action –
words were never meant to be simply admired.

Believe in putting ideas into practice –
ideas without practice are empty; practice without ideas is
    blind.

Believe in walking the walk –
it's not enough to just talk the talk.

Believe in practicing what you preach –
so what you preach is credible and encouraging.

Believe in living what you teach –
to give yourself integrity and authenticity.

~ Believe

Peace

Believe in peace –
the absence of fighting and war.

Believe in peace –
the fruit of virtue and right action.

Believe in peace –
the fruit of justice and right relations.

Believe in peace –
the end of prejudice, discrimination, and racism.

Believe in peace –
ultimately the fruit of right living and the blessing of God.

~ Believe

Making a Difference

Believe that you can improve things within you –
you have the capability to do so.

Believe that you can change things around you –
you have the ability to make things happen.

Believe that you can assist in situations –
you have a responsibility to help.

Believe that you can make the world a better place –
everything you do has an effect on things around you.

Believe that you can make a difference –
any good you do indeed makes a difference.

~ Believe

Balance

Believe in balancing your work and your recreation –
too much of one or an extreme is not healthy.

Believe in balancing together time and alone time –
we need to foster relationships and nurture ourselves.

Believe in balancing being serious and being jovial –
and we ought to know when to manifest each.

Believe in balancing being tough and being gentle –
life's many situations demand and call forth both.

Believe in balance in all its ways and aspects –
it is important in our pursuit of personal growth, peace and
  happiness.

~ Believe

Be Gentle

Believe in not being demanding –
demands reveal your lack of patience.

Believe in not being forceful –
force displays your lack of respect.

Believe in not being imposing –
imposition demonstrates your self-centeredness.

Believe in being mindful of others –
others are meant to enjoy their freedom and dignity.

Believe in being gentle with others –
others have their own thoughts, feelings, needs, and desires.

~ Believe

Passion

Believe in passion –
intense feelings for a person, cause, or task.

Believe in passion –
great energy to complete great things.

Believe in passion –
deep and abiding interest in something.

Believe in passion –
however, do not let it rule or ruin you.

Believe in passion –
and channel the energy and emotion for good!

~ Believe

~ Believe in Yourself ~

Your Own Person

Believe in your aspirations and dreams –
you have your own hopes to fulfill.

Believe in your thoughts and ideas –
you have your own mind to exercise.

Believe in your vision and future –
you have your own life to live.

Believe in your journey and odyssey –
you have your own path to follow.

Believe in your personal story and life –
you are your own person.

~ Believe

Personal Change

Believe in change –
the type you can bring about yourself.

Believe in second chances –
we all deserve a new beginning.

Believe in healing –
the inner kind with lasting effects.

Believe in improvement –
it all begins with positive thinking.

Believe in personal transformation –
it is more attainable than you think.

~ Believe

Believe in Self

Believe in self-confidence –
have faith in yourself and your abilities.

Believe in self-esteem –
respect and like yourself.

Believe in self-reliance –
you are able and capable.

Believe in self-worth –
you are good and you are loveable.

Believe in self-motivation –
you can do it!

~ Believe

Self-improvement

Believe in character,
the fluid inner working of our person we develop.

Believe in integrity,
the solid center core of our being we hold on to.

Believe in good,
the underlying moral principle of our life.

Believe in virtue,
the good habits, attitudes, and actions we adhere to.

Believe in holiness,
the striving for spiritual excellence and perfection.

~ Believe

You Are Good, Capable, and Loveable

Believe that you are good in your nature and being –
that's the way you were made.

Believe that you are able to love –
it is a power you are endowed with.

Believe that you capable of knowing truth –
it is the proper object of your intellect.

Believe that you are loveable –
it is natural to love that which is good.

Believe that you are good, able, capable, and loveable –
simply because it is true.

~ Believe

Be Positive

Believe that some illnesses can be cured –
remain positive and optimistic in your condition.

Believe that much sickness can be overcome –
have patience and allow nature to run its course.

Believe that addiction can be beaten –
resolve to change, take small steps, and don't quit.

Believe that depression can be relieved –
get help, support, rest, exercise, and nutrition.

Believe that negativity can be improved –
change your attitude and be positive!

~ Believe

Be Yourself

Believe that wild horses must run free –
that is their activity by nature and they must do it.

Believe that a runner must run –
he is an athlete by nature and must run to be at peace.

Believe that a singer must sing –
she possesses this natural gift and must sing to be happy.

Believe that a writer must write –
he has this natural ability and must write to be fulfilled.

Believe that you must be your positive natural self –
because in doing so you will be happy and at peace.

~ Believe

You Are Special

Believe that you are special, unique and one of a kind –
there has never existed anyone just like you.

Believe that you are good in your person and nature –
in every fiber and ounce of your being.

Believe that you possess immense value and worth –
and carry with you fundamental human dignity and respect.

Believe that God made you out of love –
and holds you and all things in existence.

Believe in celebrating your existence and unique self –
also acknowledge and honor God who made and loves you!

~ Believe

Your Spiritual Nature

Believe in being a spiritual person,
living and acting according to your spiritual nature.

Believe in being a spiritual athlete,
working, training, and striving for spiritual excellence.

Believe in being a spiritual giant,
being virtuous and moving towards holiness and sanctity.

Believe in being a spiritual warrior,
strategizing, mobilizing, and fighting for good over evil.

Believe in being a spiritual person,
truly fulfilling yourself and realizing your true nature.

~ Believe

Believe in Yourself

Believe in your fundamental goodness and dignity –
in virtue of being made in the image and likeness of God.

Believe in your inherent value and worth –
you possess it simply because you are a human being.

Believe in your distinct uniqueness and being special –
there never was nor will there ever be someone just like you.

Believe in your gifts, talents, and abilities –
you have much potential waiting to be actualized.

Believe in your importance –
you have your place and mark to be made in this world.

~ Believe

~ Greater and Beyond ~

Believe With Your Whole Being

Believe with your whole heart,
in everything that is good.

Believe with your whole mind,
in everything that is true.

Believe with all your senses,
in everything that is beautiful.

Believe with all your will,
in everything that is important.

Believe with your whole being,
in everything worth believing.

~ Believe

Beyond Yourself

Believe in a world outside yourself –
it leads to truth and knowing what is true.

Believe in people other than yourself –
it leads to love and being a loving person.

Believe in possibilities higher than yourself –
it leads to hope and being truly hopeful.

Believe in things beyond yourself –
it leads to happiness and being happy.

Believe in a power greater than yourself –
it leads to God and living a God-centered life.

~ Believe

Possibilities

Believe in your dreams,
but don't build castles in the sky.

Believe in your abilities,
but don't forget your limitations.

Believe in your strengths,
but don't forget your weaknesses.

Believe in yourself,
but don't become self-centered.

Believe in the possibilities,
but don't forget the realities.

~ Believe

Thinking Outside the Box

Believe in going beyond your comfort zone –
you will grow and learn through discomfort.

Believe in feeling more than safety and security –
you will also thrive in risk and adventure.

Believe in doing greater than the status quo –
you can go beyond mediocrity and the norm.

Believe in achieving higher than the average –
you can accomplish more if you simply try.

Believe in thinking outside the box –
you will see things you didn't see before.

~ Believe

Potential and Power

Believe in heightened awareness –
open up all your faculties and powers.

Believe in deeper knowledge –
constantly look below the surface of things.

Believe in broader understanding –
look up and down and sideways.

Believe in profound wisdom –
integration and synthesis gives us deeper understanding.

Believe in the potential and power of the human mind –
to know, understand, judge, and be enlightened.

~ Believe

Higher Consciousness

Believe in personal transformation,
the kind where we make life altering changes.

Believe in peak experiences,
the kind that leaves us with lasting impressions.

Believe in clarity of vision,
the kind of profound seeing that moves us to tears.

Believe in illumination,
the kind of enlightenment that lights up our world.

Believe in higher states of consciousness,
the kind attainable by the persevering seeker.

~ Believe

Beyond the Senses

Believe in your eyes,
but close them and see with the eyes of your heart.

Believe in your ears,
but cover them and hear the golden silence within your soul.

Believe in your nose,
but hold it and experience the sweet smell of success.

Believe in your taste,
but deny it and savor the richness of spiritual nourishment.

Believe in your touch,
but suspend it and feel the inner joy deep within your soul.

~ Believe

Strive For Higher and Better

Believe in excelling beyond the ordinary –
you will raise yourself to new levels.

Believe in pushing yourself to the limit –
you will realize you can do more than you thought.

Believe in challenging yourself to new things –
you will open up new opportunities for yourself.

Believe in doing greater than what is expected –
you will experience the joy of success.

Believe in striving for higher and better –
you will accomplish and achieve many things.

~ Believe

Greater and Beyond

Believe in a world,
broader than your present horizon.

Believe in a love,
greater than your limited experience.

Believe in a vision,
beyond your present sight.

Believe in a wisdom,
larger than your current understanding.

Believe in a myriad of realities,
greater and beyond your imposed limitations.

~ Believe

~ Human Beings ~

Significant Others

Believe in those who trust you –
they will reveal your solid integrity.

Believe in those who respect you –
they will reveal your true character.

Believe in those who value you –
they will reveal your inherent worth.

Believe in those who love you –
they will reveal your authentic goodness.

Believe in those who believe in you –
they will reveal your real potential.

~ Believe

Multifaceted Beings

Believe that we are social beings –
our most significant things in life involve other people.

Believe that we are emotional beings –
our feelings reflect our mental, physical, and attitudinal states.

Believe that we are physical beings –
our bodies tie us down to time and place and ground us.

Believe that we are mental beings –
we have the capacity to know, understand, reason and judge.

Believe that we are spiritual beings –
we can transcend the physical and connect with God.

~ Believe

Parents

Believe in your parents –
you would not be here if it wasn't for them.

Believe in your parents –
even though they are not perfect.

Believe in your parents –
they deserve your respect and gratitude.

Believe in your parents –
they are your roots and hopefully they've given you wings.

Believe in your parents –
whom God has chosen for you and you for them.

~ Believe

Children

Believe in your children –
they are yours forever.

Believe in your children –
they have been entrusted to your temporal care.

Believe in your children –
feed, clothe, and nurture them.

Believe in your children –
form and develop them into their own person.

Believe in your children, who come from God –
show them the way back to God.

~ Believe

Family

Believe in family,
both a physical and spiritual reality.

Believe in family,
the basic cell and fundamental building block of society.

Believe in family,
where we grow, develop, learn and experience.

Believe in family,
where we feel connected, related, and a sense of belonging.

Believe in family,
one of the most important entities in life, society,
     and the world.

~ Believe

One Human Family

Believe in God –
we are all children of one Creator.

Believe in friends –
they are connections and relations.

Believe in family –
it is our root and support system.

Believe in acquaintances –
they enrich us by their very being.

Believe in people –
we are all one human family together under God.

~ Believe

Personhood

Believe in the small, unborn baby –
the future of society and the human race.

Believe in the young, growing child –
innocent, active and energetic.

Believe in the developing, emerging adolescent –
in transition, searching for identity.

Believe in the older, experienced adult –
practical wisdom, knowledge, and understanding.

Believe in the wonder of each human person –
we come in all shapes and sizes, ages and stages.

~ Believe

Self-centeredness

Believe that most people think primarily,
for their own well-being and enjoyment.

Believe that most people do things primarily,
for their own gain and satisfaction.

Believe that all people are self-centered to some degree,
for this flows from our fallen human nature.

Believe that we must attend to our own needs and wishes,
but not to the exclusion and disregard of others.

Believe that we are to overcome our flawed human nature,
and love our neighbor as we would love ourselves.

~ Believe

Human Beings

Believe that we are spiritual beings,
living in a material world.

Believe that we are eternal beings,
living in a temporal world.

Believe that we wish for perfection,
but we live in an imperfect world.

Believe that we wish for authentic and permanent love,
only to experience it fragmented and limited.

Believe that human beings are indeed odd creatures,
able to sink lower than brute animals and rise higher than the
    angels.

~ Believe

Physical and Spiritual Beings

Believe that all material things,
are subject to time and space.

Believe that our physical nature,
confines us to a specific time in a specific place.

Believe that all immaterial things,
are not subject to the laws that govern material things.

Believe that our spiritual nature,
can rise, transcend, and soar far and beyond the physical.

Believe that we are both physical and spiritual beings,
however, it is the human soul that resembles the Divine.

~ Believe

~ Things Human ~

Distinctly Human

Believe in a sincere smile,
a simple thing with big results.

Believe in pleasant surprises,
the little unexpected joys of life.

Believe in positive humor,
the distinctly human twist to the ordinary.

Believe in genuine laughter,
the infectious sound of human spontaneity.

Believe in wholesome fun,
the free and happy child in us all.

~ Believe

Human Necessities

Believe in exercise and nutrition –
necessary for a healthy body.

Believe in silence and reflection –
necessary for a healthy mind.

Believe in sharing and venting –
necessary for healthy emotions.

Believe in love and laughter –
necessary for a healthy heart.

Believe in prayer and meditation –
necessary for a healthy soul.

~ Believe

Basic Human Desires

Believe that all persons have similar basic needs –
for all of us share the same human nature created by God.

Believe that everyone desires to be acknowledged –
"I am here… I am somebody… I have a name."

Believe that everyone desires to be known and esteemed –
"Know who I am… Please understand me… I am special."

Believe that everyone desires to be affirmed and loved –
"I am good… I need you… Please love me."

Believe that everyone desires to be happy and at peace –
"I want to be happy… I want to feel secure… I want peace."

~ Believe

Desire

Believe that all humans have desires, wants, and needs,
revealing that human nature is incomplete and wanting.

Believe that people desire the good they are attracted to,
according to sense, appetite, emotion, intellect, and will.

Believe that all people desire fulfillment and happiness,
and this is the fundamental motivation in all we do.

Believe that human desire is fundamentally good,
in so far as it is ordered to its proper object and end.

Believe that underlying all desire is really desire for God,
our ultimate good, fulfillment, goal, object, and end.

~ Believe

Freedom

Believe in free will,
however, it doesn't imply absolute freedom and license.

Believe in free choice,
however, there are good choices, and there are bad choices.

Believe in free decisions,
however, you have a duty and obligation to be responsible
    for good.

Believe in freedom,
one of the characteristics that makes us truly human.

Believe in God's gift of freedom to us,
and the good we do with it is our gift to God.

~ *Believe*

Human Broken-ness

Believe that many people lead lives of quiet desperation –
anxious, dissatisfied, unhappy, and unfulfilled.

Believe that many people suffer much internally –
loneliness, hopelessness, depression, and despair.

Believe that many individuals are broken –
hurts, wounds, pain, and loss.

Believe that many relationships are broken –
betrayal, division, separation, and cessation.

Believe that there is much human broken-ness –
however, there is always hope with God who helps and heals.

~ Believe

Pleasure and Pain

Believe that some people always seek pleasure and avoid pain,
and much of their lives revolve around this philosophy.

Believe that pleasure is a God-given good,
however, it must be tempered and ordered properly.

Believe that pain is a part of life we all experience,
and one of the secrets of life is how to suffer well for growth.

Believe that pleasure and pain is only a part of living,
and they are physically rooted and experienced.

Believe that the higher part of our nature is spiritual,
where we have the more profound realities of joy and suffering.

~ Believe

Sex and Sexuality

Believe that sex is what you do,
and sexuality is part of who you are.

Believe that the purpose of sex,
is love and procreation, babies and bonding.

Believe that sexuality has profound meaning,
in the differentiation and complementary nature of male and
   female.

Believe that the proper place for sex is marriage,
where love is fostered and babies are welcome.

Believe that sex and sexuality are fundamentally good,
gifts from God for our individual and collective good.

~ Believe

Inner Beauty

Believe in inner beauty,
a beauty greater than external good looks.

Believe in inner beauty,
the attractive state of your spirit and soul.

Believe in inner beauty,
a combination of disposition, attitude, and virtue.

Believe in inner beauty,
where character and personality are important.

Believe in the inner beauty of spirit and soul,
where God can beautify us all.

~ Believe

Things Depend on You

Believe that we basically get out of life,
what we basically put into it.

Believe that the quality of our relationships,
is directly related to the effort we devote to them.

Believe that our happiness and inner peace,
hinges largely upon our thinking and attitude.

Believe that our success and fulfillment,
depend much upon our actions and behavior.

Believe that our ultimate and eternal destiny with God,
is a joint human and divine effort and endeavor.

~ Believe

Personal Destiny

Believe in purpose –
it gives significance and meaning to all we do.

Believe in meaning –
it helps us make sense of everything.

Believe in fulfillment –
it is something we all want.

Believe in happiness –
it is something we all desire.

Believe in personal destiny –
it is something we work out as we go.

~ Believe

Friendship

Believe in the loyalty of a friend,
always being there for you, in good times and in bad.

Believe in the companionship of a friend,
sharing common interests and doing things together.

Believe in the confidence of a friend,
barring your soul and venting your feelings freely.

Believe in the respect of a friend,
being yourself in your strengths and weaknesses.

Believe in the love of a friend,
desiring the best and doing good for each other.

~ Believe

Human Life

Believe that life is the fundamental good –
without it, there can be no other goods to have and hold.

Believe that life is the fundamental right –
without it, there can be no other rights to enjoy.

Believe that life is to be lived –
such is the profound and fertile nature of life.

Believe that human life is valuable and precious –
each one meant to be valued and cherished.

Believe that human life is God-given and sacred –
everyone intended to be protected and respected always.

~ Believe

Cycles of Life

Believe in the cycle of life –
we are conceived, born, live, die, and then live forever.

Believe in the cycle of care –
we are cared for, and then we care for our caregivers.

Believe in the cycle of love –
love begets love and love comes back to those who love.

Believe in the cycle of truth –
truth always comes back in some way, shape, or form.

Believe in the cycle of existence –
we come from God, we live, and then we go back to God.

~ Believe

~ Relationship ~

Believe in Her

Believe in the female spirit,
the perfect human complement to the male animus.

Believe in femininity,
the distinctive heart, soul, body and mind of personhood.

Believe in her needs,
and her desire to feel special and appreciated.

Believe in her mystery,
and in her unique beauty unto herself.

Believe in her,
and watch a marvel unfold before your eyes.

~ Believe

Believe in Him

Believe in the male animus,
the perfect human complement to the female spirit.

Believe in masculinity,
the distinctive heart, soul, body and mind of personhood.

Believe in his needs,
and his desire to feel useful and important.

Believe in his driving force,
and in his enigma even to himself.

Believe in him,
and watch him accomplish many things.

~ Believe

Special and Loving Relationship

Believe in a special relationship,
and the complementary nature of male and female.

Believe in the connecting of two separate individuals,
with their different and unique characters and personalities.

Believe in the merging together as one,
all the while remaining distinct and free.

Believe in closeness and intimacy,
the baring of minds, hearts, bodies, and souls.

Believe in a loving relationship,
loving and being loved in return – a wonderful and beautiful
   thing!

~ Believe

Her Uniqueness

Believe in her smile,
as it catches your eye and makes you pause.

Believe in her eyes,
as their sparkle turns your head and makes you look.

Believe in her walk,
as it captures your attention and makes you want to follow.

Believe in her warmth,
as it invites you and draws you nearer.

Believe in her goodness and beauty,
and see more to her than what first meets the eye.

~ Believe

His Uniqueness

Believe in his smile –
it's natural and sincere.

Believe in his eyes –
look closely and see yourself revealed in them.

Believe in his movement –
it's confident and with purpose.

Believe in his sincere intentions –
as they invite you and draw you closer.

Believe in his character –
there is more to him than his feelings of affection.

~ Believe

Soul Mate

Believe in a wonderful friend,
one with whom you connect on many levels.

Believe in a special person,
one with whom you are special to each other.

Believe in a unique individual,
one who is not like any other for you.

Believe in that one person,
one to whom you can give your all.

Believe in a soul mate,
the one it seems you were made for.

~ Believe

Your Spouse

Believe in commitment to your spouse,
staying with them through difficulty and hardship.

Believe in loyalty to your spouse,
being there for them in all their needs.

Believe in fidelity to your spouse,
being faithful to them in mind, heart, and body.

Believe in devotion to your spouse,
having that extra special attitude toward them.

Believe in your spouse,
for only in believing in each other will you be happy together.

~ Believe

Marriage

Believe in marriage,
the love and mystical union of two distinct individuals.

Believe in marriage,
the love and permanent commitment of each for the other.

Believe in marriage,
the love and profound respect for each other.

Believe in marriage,
the institution that is so basic, necessary, and important.

Believe in marriage,
the sacrament of matrimony, greater than the sum of two
     individuals.

~ Believe

Being in Love

Believe in one very special person,
with whom you can be in love with.

Believe in one very special relationship,
in which you both connect deeply and attract greatly.

Believe in one very special friend and companion,
with whom you mutually respect and trust.

Believe in very special times with each other,
when you are both smiling and so happy.

Believe in being in love,
with the right chemistry, right timing, and right person!

~ Believe

Important Things in Relationships

Believe in trust,
the ties which join us to each other.

Believe in commitment,
the mortar which bonds us together.

Believe in respect,
the foundation on which we build.

Believe in freedom,
the room and space which we both need.

Believe in selflessness,
the special ingredient in any relationship.

~ Believe

~ Important Things ~

Small and Enjoyable Things

Believe in the small enjoyable things in life –
in which we are able to experience real joy.

Believe in enjoying a great cup of coffee –
while reading a new and captivating book.

Believe in enjoying nature in all its grandeur –
the sights, the sounds, and the tangible experience.

Believe in enjoying family events with your children –
the special times you cherish in your heart forever.

*Believe in human joy that nurtures the spirit and warms
    the soul –*
a spiritual response to a physical event.

~ Believe

True Spirit of Christmas

Believe in the true Spirit of Christmas,
the love, the peace, and the joy.

Believe in the true Spirit of Christmas,
the good will, the forgiveness, and the reconciliation.

Believe in the true Spirit of Christmas,
the family, the friends, and the relatives.

Believe in the true Spirit of Christmas,
the serving, the giving, and the receiving.

Believe in the true Spirit of Christmas,
the promise, the Savior, and the hope of the world.

~ Believe

Believe

Believe in an end to pain and suffering,
and a time of health and happiness.

Believe in an end to disappointment and sadness,
and a time of optimism and joy.

Believe in an end to betrayal and separation,
and a time of trust and union.

Believe in an end to aggression and depression,
and a time of peace and happiness.

Believe in an end to skepticism and doubt,
and a time of truth and faith.

~ Believe

Keep Believing

Believe in your family,
even when you are not on good terms with them.

Believe in your friends,
even when you don't feel their support.

Believe in your colleagues,
even when they do not cooperate with you.

Believe in yourself,
even when you suffer from self-doubt.

Believe in God,
even when you don't feel or sense God's presence.

~ Believe

Sharing

Believe that by joining your suffering with another,
your suffering will decrease.

Believe that by sharing your joy with another,
your joy will increase.

Believe that by sharing your work with another,
your toil will seem much less than half.

Believe that by sharing your good fortune with another,
fortune will come back to you.

Believe that by sharing yourself and what you have,
you will be all the richer and enriched.

~ Believe

Acceptance

Believe in and accept suffering,
and all the growth that can be experienced.

Believe in and accept hardship,
and all the insight that can be gained.

Believe in and accept pain,
and all the enlightenment that can be attained.

Believe in and accept discomfort,
and all the benefits that can be derived.

Believe in and accept sacrifice,
and all the good that can result.

~ Believe

Letting Go

Believe in letting go of control –
people and life are not meant to be controlled.

Believe in letting go of bad habits –
they are only destructive to you.

Believe in letting go of the need for predictability –
you are limiting yourself to other and greater possibilities.

Believe in letting go of manipulation –
let people and their lives unfold as they should.

Believe in letting go of anything unhealthy –
you owe it to yourself and to others.

~ Believe

Service

Believe in yourself and serve yourself –
you have to attend to your needs.

Believe in others and serve them –
there is much we can do to help and assist.

Believe in God and serve Him –
we have His Commandments and Will to follow.

Believe in service and serving –
a basic calling and duty in life.

Believe in service to God, others, and self –
God is first, others are second, and self is third.

~ Believe

Priorities

Believe that people are more important than things –
love people and use things, not the other way around.

Believe that the spiritual is more valuable than the material –
the spirit is eternal whereas the material is passing.

Believe that loving is greater than knowing –
God judges us on how loving we are, not how smart.

Believe that giving is nobler than receiving –
ironically, it's the giver who actually receives the most.

Believe that God is the most important of all –
in our essential believing, God is absolutely central.

~ Believe

Reconciliation

Believe in apology –
admitting your offense and saying you are sorry.

Believe in forgiveness –
letting go of the offense and releasing the person.

Believe in reconciling –
one apologizes, one forgives, and two are reconciled.

Believe in reconciliation with God –
we must be sorry with a contrite heart; God is always willing
    to forgive.

Believe in apology, forgiveness, and reconciliation –
cause for joy, and a blessing of God!

~ Believe

Working Together

Believe in teamwork –
it's how we share the work.

Believe in cooperation –
it's how we work together.

Believe in networking –
it's how we help each other.

Believe in collaboration –
it's how we work things out.

Believe in the common good –
your good and my good is our good.

~ Believe

Important Things

Believing gives us vision –
without a vision, we are blind.

Believing gives us direction –
without a path, we are lost.

Believing gives us goals –
without a goal, our efforts are futile.

Believing gives us inspiration, energy, and resolve –
without these, we give up and falter.

Believing gives us God –
without God, we are left to own our devices and doomed
     to fail.

~ Believe

~ Basic Things ~

Unity of All Things

Believe in the harmony of life –
the result of right order and peaceful relations.

Believe in the balance of nature –
calling us to stewardship and respect of the environment.

Believe in the integration of living –
elements brought together for health and happiness.

Believe in the interrelationships of people –
we are all interrelated and interconnected.

Believe in the unity of all things –
everything is part of the whole and significant in some way.

~ Believe

The Objective World

Believe that you are part of the universe,
not the center of it.

Believe that truth is determined by reality,
and so are you.

Believe that there is a whole world existing outside of you,
and your real subjective experience is not the only world.

Believe that it is of utmost importance,
to make a healthy response to the objective world.

Believe that one of the keys to happiness,
is integrating well the subjective and objective elements.

~ Believe

Falsehoods and Lies

Believe that the minds of people and the world,
are full of falsehoods, lies, deceptions and frauds.

Believe that the first lies concern spiritual realties,
that God, angels, and the devil don't really exist.

Believe that the next lies concern human beings,
that persons do not possess an immaterial and immortal soul.

Believe that further lies concern our ability to know truth,
that we are incapable of attaining truth beyond the physical.

Believe that other lies concern our ability to love,
that altruistic and purely motivated love is not possible.

~ Believe

Fundamental Things

Believe in values –
those things you value and cherish.

Believe in principles –
those beliefs you anchor yourself to.

Believe in ideals –
those ideas which lift and raise you up.

Believe in morals –
those judgments which guide and direct your actions.

Believe in right –
the values, principles, ideals, and morals that center you.

~ Believe

Life

Believe that the path of life is like a long journey –
make sure you journey to God and arrive there safely.

Believe that the course of life is like one big adventure –
let God make it all the more adventurous.

Believe that the events of life are meant to be challenges –
accept all the challenges God gives, and learn and grow.

Believe that the path, course, and events of our lives –
become individual odysseys and personal stories.

Believe that with God alongside of us –
everything is as good as it will ever get in this life.

~ Believe

Grace and Nature

Believe that God profoundly respects our intellects,
allowing us to discover things on our own.

Believe that God profoundly respects our freedom,
allowing us to make choices and decisions.

Believe that God helps us while respecting our nature,
allowing us to be and act according to our unique character.

Believe that God gives us His life and grace,
allowing us to grow spiritually and be transformed.

Believe that divine grace builds upon human nature,
not overpower or take anything away from it.

~ Believe

Unless

Believe that love remains just an ideal,
unless we live it and demonstrate it in practice and action.

Believe that truth remains just a concept,
unless we speak it, teach it, and make it come alive.

Believe that faith remains just a set of beliefs,
unless we are truly converted, convicted, and committed.

Believe that good remains just a word,
unless we truly value it and actually do good.

Believe that God remains just a vague abstraction,
unless we sense the power and love of God within and
    around us.

~ Believe

Power

Believe in the energizing power of love –
filled with it, we have zeal and energy.

Believe in the imperative power of truth –
knowing it, we are compelled to act according to it.

Believe in the inspiring power of goodness –
seeing it, we want and desire to do good.

Believe in the persevering power of faith –
possessing it, we overcome many obstacles.

Believe in the almighty power of God –
tapping into it, we become stronger.

~ Believe

Perception

Believe that reality is something real and objective,
something to be known as true by the human intellect.

Believe that our individual perceptions,
don't necessarily correspond to objective reality.

Believe that clear water in a blue glass,
only appears to be blue, but is not actually blue.

Believe that seeing things through rose colored glasses,
does not mean everything is nice and rosy.

Believe that whatever is perceived by a person,
is perceived according to the mode, manner, and state of the
    individual.

~ Believe

Momentous Times

Believe that we are living in momentous times –
world events are large in scope and impact.

Believe that we are witnessing things never before seen –
just open your eyes and look around.

Believe that we are living on the brink of disaster –
we are in big trouble in so many ways.

Believe that we are being called back to God –
to live and love as we ought.

Believe that the great mercy of God –
is withholding His judgment and justice for all.

~ Believe

Origin of the Human Species

Believe that the origin of the human species,
is a large and important question.

Believe that the answer is alarmingly simple,
for God is the creator of all things without exception.

Believe that how God created humans is another question,
the answer to which we have different ideas and theories.

Believe that whatever the theory, truth dictates to all,
and the first truth is God governs the process of creation.

Believe that truth does not contradict itself,
and fault always lies on the part of human error.

~ Believe

Science

Believe in science and its origins –
it comes from a Latin word meaning to know.

Believe in science and its method –
we study the physical, observable, and measurable.

Believe in science and its products –
it gives us inventions and technology for our good.

Believe in science and its scope –
and keep it within its proper bounds and limits.

Believe in science and its proper place –
and acknowledge God, the author and creator of the
    physical world.

~ Believe

Basic Things

Believe in love, the energizing force of life –
without it, we would not have zest and zeal.

Believe in faith, the direction and vision of life –
without it, we would falter and flounder.

Believe in hope, the light and optimism of life –
without it, we would live in the shadows of pessimism.

Believe in joy, the gift of life –
without it, the world would be very grey and dreary.

Believe in peace, the tranquility and order of life –
without it, the world would be disordered and chaotic.

~ Believe

Made For a Purpose

Believe that your mind was made for truth –
only with truth will you be satisfied.

Believe that your heart was made for love –
only with love will you be at peace.

Believe that your spirit was made for happiness –
only with happiness will you be fulfilled.

Believe that your soul was made for God –
only with God will you be at rest.

Believe that you were made for a purpose –
only with life's purpose will you find life's true meaning.

~ Believe

Called For a Purpose

Believe in quest –
we are all searching for something.

Believe in mission –
we all have a purpose to accomplish.

Believe in task –
we all have an important job to complete.

Believe in calling –
we all have our individual part to do.

Believe in plan –
God has a special plan for each and every one of us.

~ Believe

~ Transcendent Things ~

Actual Truth

Believe in actual truth,
as opposed to opinion, convention, or majority vote.

Believe in actual truth,
as opposed to societal norms and cultural customs.

Believe in actual truth,
as opposed to family traditions and accepted notions.

Believe in actual truth,
as opposed to popular belief and unsubstantiated claims.

Believe in actual truth,
the correspondence of a subject's mind to objective reality.

~ Believe

Authentic Love

Believe in authentic love,
as opposed to emotionalism and feelings only.

Believe in authentic love,
as opposed to infatuation and wrapped up in self.

Believe in authentic love,
as opposed to unhealthy need and dependence on the other.

Believe in authentic love,
as opposed to underlying control and manipulation of
    the other.

Believe in authentic love,
the doing and being for the other for their true good.

~ Believe

Grounded Faith

Believe in grounded faith,
as opposed to fancy notions and esoteric imaginings.

Believe in grounded faith,
as opposed to individual projection of wants and desires.

Believe in grounded faith,
as opposed to a blind passive response to something given.

Believe in grounded faith,
and always have an answer for what you believe.

Believe in grounded faith,
the stepping out and beyond, while staying connected to what
   is real and true.

~ Believe

True Good

Believe in the true good,
as opposed to apparent and false goods.

Believe in the true good,
as opposed to opinions as to what is good.

Believe in the true good,
as opposed to a purely subjective good.

Believe in the true good,
as opposed to skepticism in knowing it.

Believe in the true good,
the real and objective good with universal application.

~ Believe

Real Hope

Believe in real hope –
to wish for something and expect its fulfillment.

Believe in real hope –
to desire a future good and wait for its securing.

Believe in real hope –
to trust in a positive outcome with confidence.

Believe in real hope –
to hold your aspirations with patience and perseverance.

Believe in real hope –
the wishing, desiring, trusting, and holding, all with positive
expectation.

~ Believe

Essential Things

Believe in actual truth –
the correspondence of a subject's mind to objective reality.

Believe in authentic love –
the doing and being for the other for their good.

Believe in grounded faith –
the stepping out and beyond, while staying connected to what
    is real and true.

Believe in true good –
the real and objective good with universal application.

Believe in real hope –
the wishing, desiring, trusting, and holding, all with positive
    expectation.

~ Believe

Believe in Truth

Believe in truth,
the deep yearning of the soul, and proper object of
    the intellect.

Believe in truth,
the beautiful and awesome correspondence of mind
    and reality.

Believe in truth,
and in the different ways of coming to know it.

Believe in truth,
even though it loves to hide and waits to be discovered.

Believe in truth,
something beyond the realm of subjective opinion.

~ Believe

Possession of Truth

Believe in arriving at truth,
through the senses and our experience of the physical.

Believe in arriving at truth,
through the intellect and our exercise of reason and logic.

Believe in arriving at truth,
through the sense of profound intuition and deep gut feeling.

Believe in arriving at truth,
through the common and trusted experience of human living.

Believe in arriving at truth,
through Divine illumination and faith in God's revelation.

~ Believe

Discovering Truth

Believe in discovering truth,
hidden behind the curtain of our indifference.

Believe in discovering truth,
obscured behind the veil of our pride.

Believe in discovering truth,
darkened by the shadows of our sinfulness.

Believe in discovering truth,
blinded by our self-centeredness and selfishness.

Believe in discovering truth,
as we continue our journey to God, Who is Truth.

~ Believe

Truth

Believe that truth is found in many forms and fields –
reality is rich and so is truth.

Believe that truth has internal integrity and objectivity –
truth is correspondence to reality.

Believe that when two things are at odds or different –
both cannot be true at the same time in the same respect.

Believe that truth does not contradict itself –
human error creates and produces contradictions.

Believe that religion and science were not meant to be at odds –
true religion and true science are compatible by nature.

~ Believe

The Greatness of Love

Believe in love and all its positive forms and types –
it is such a varied and rich thing.

Believe in love and all its power and force –
it can melt hearts and transform lives.

Believe in love and all its beauty and grandeur –
it is the highest and greatest of relationships.

Believe in love and all its allure and desire –
it is the deepest and strongest desire of the human heart.

Believe in love and all its wonder and greatness –
the secret of the universe, the way to God, and the path to
     happiness.

~ Believe

True Love

Believe that true love is genuine –
it is real and authentic.

Believe that true love is altruistic –
it truly loves the other and is blind to self.

Believe that true love is sacrificial –
it gives up self and things for the other.

Believe that true love seeks the good –
it desires and works for the good of the other.

Believe that true love reflects the nature of God –
for God is Love.

~ Believe

True Satisfaction

Believe in the beauty of truth –
truth truly satisfies the thirst of the intellect.

Believe in the beauty of love –
love truly satisfies the longing of the heart.

Believe in the beauty of faith –
faith truly satisfies the yearning of the soul.

Believe in the beauty of hope –
hope truly satisfies the anxiety of the spirit.

Believe in the beauty of God –
God truly and ultimately satisfies all and everything.

~ Believe

~ Life of the Spirit ~

The Cardinal Virtues

Believe in prudence –
doing the right thing at the right time.

Believe in temperance –
moderating one's desires, attractions, and passions.

Believe in fortitude –
inner strength in the face of hardship and difficulty.

Believe in justice –
giving to others what they need and deserve.

Believe in these fundamental cardinal virtues –
they help us develop all other virtues.

~ Believe

The Theological Virtues

Believe in the theological virtue of faith –
it enables us to believe God and all that God reveals to us.

Believe in the theological virtue of hope –
it moves us to desire and trust in heaven and eternal
    happiness.

Believe in the theological virtue of love –
it empowers us to love God above all and our neighbor as
    ourselves.

Believe in the theological virtues –
God-given virtues we cannot gain by our own efforts.

Believe in faith, hope, and love –
essential for our life, happiness, and eternal destiny.

~ Believe

Gifts of The Holy Spirit

Believe in wisdom, knowledge, and understanding,
gifts of the Spirit for our minds and judgment.

Believe in counsel,
gift of the Spirit for guidance and direction.

Believe in fortitude,
gift of the Spirit for courage and strength.

Believe in piety and fear of the Lord,
gifts of the Spirit to help us become holy.

Believe in the Gifts of the Holy Spirit,
gifts to nourish and satisfy our spiritual nature.

~ Believe

Fruits of The Holy Spirit

Believe in love, joy, and peace –
qualities we possess within, radiating out to others.

Believe in patience, kindness, and goodness –
virtues we extend to others through our actions.

Believe in faithfulness, gentleness, and self-control –
dispositions we display through our behavior.

Believe in the fruits of the Spirit –
living these fruits, we are better and happier people.

Believe in the fruits of the Holy Spirit –
fruits we enjoy when we let the Spirit of God direct our lives.

~ Believe

The Beatitudes

Believe in the Beatitudes –
a teaching of Jesus to his disciples and the crowd.

Believe in the Beatitudes –
lessons on how to be, act, and live life.

Believe in the Beatitudes –
a blessing and promise of true happiness.

Believe in the Beatitudes –
blessed are those who are as Jesus describes.

Believe in the Beatitudes –
sure stepping stones on the path to heaven.

~ Believe

Spiritual Power

Believe in the power of truth –
it can illuminate the darkest of minds.

Believe in the power of love –
it can move the hardest of hearts.

Believe in the power of hope –
it can overcome the depths of despair.

Believe in the power of faith –
it connects us to the greatest truths of life.

Believe in the power of God –
it ultimately answers and gives us everything.

~ Believe

Repentance

Believe that humans are not perfect,
in any way, shape or form.

Believe that we are all sinners,
not doing the good we know we ought to do.

Believe that we must acknowledge our faults and failings,
before God who knows every intention and act.

Believe that we must go before God with a contrite heart,
and be sorry and confess our wrongdoings.

Believe that we must repent of all our sins,
and make atonement for all our transgressions.

~ Believe

Prayer

Believe that communication with God,
is possible, important, and necessary.

Believe that prayer in its simplest form,
is an interaction of talking and listening to God.

Believe that in prayer,
we raise our minds, hearts, and souls to God.

Believe that through prayer,
we make a real connection with God and His will for us.

Believe that prayer has power,
and combined with faith, it can "move mountains."

~ Believe

The Works of Mercy

Believe in the corporal works of mercy –
give food to the hungry, drink to the thirsty,
      clothes to the naked.

Believe in the corporal works of mercy –
welcome the stranger, visit the sick and imprisoned,
      bury the dead.

Believe in the spiritual works of mercy –
counsel the doubtful, instruct the ignorant,
      admonish the sinner.

Believe in the spiritual works of mercy –
comfort the sorrowful, bear wrongs patiently, pray for others.

Believe in the spiritual and corporal works of mercy –
help others and do it out of love.

~ Believe

The Sacraments

Believe in the Holy Sacraments,
channels of divine grace and life for human souls.

Believe in Baptism, Reconciliation, and Confirmation,
sacraments initiating us in the life of Jesus Christ.

Believe in Eucharist, the real body and blood of Jesus,
spiritual nourishment in the bread of life and cup of salvation.

Believe in Matrimony and Holy Orders,
sacraments helping us faithfully live our vocation in life.

Believe in the Blessing of the Sick,
giving us strength and health of body and soul.

~ Believe

The Hearts of Jesus and Mary

Believe in the heart of Jesus,
a Sacred Heart most loving and merciful.

Believe in the heart of Mary,
an Immaculate Heart so tender and loving.

Believe in the two hearts of the heavenly realm,
one human-divine, one human, in true union with each other.

Believe in their two hearts close to us from on high,
teaching and guiding us in the way of authentic love.

Believe in true and deep love between two human souls,
in love and imitation of the Hearts of Jesus and Mary.

~ Believe

The Cross

Believe that Jesus took up his cross –
he accepted it and carried it.

Believe that Jesus embraced the cross –
he accepted it and did the will of his Father.

Believe that we are followers of Jesus –
we also are called to accept and take up our crosses daily.

Believe that everybody has crosses in life –
they are made lighter by uniting them with Jesus' cross.

Believe that Jesus died on the cross and saved the world –
the crosses we carry play a part in God's plan of salvation.

~ Believe

Do Good, Avoid Evil

Believe that the fundamental moral imperative is,
"Do good and avoid evil."

Believe that we are called to act and behave well,
objectively and in the eyes of God.

Believe that being good and doing good,
are indeed good for self, others, society, and the world.

Believe that evil is not something in itself,
but an absence of good that ought to be present.

Believe that good will always triumph over evil in the end,
for such is the profound nature of good and of evil.

~ Believe

Being Faithful to God

Believe that being successful in life,
is not as important as being faithful to God.

Believe that being prosperous in work and business,
is not as great as being faithful to God.

Believe that being respected by others,
is not as praise worthy as being faithful to God.

Believe that being held high in esteem by friends,
is not as lofty as being faithful to God.

Believe that even being happy within oneself,
is not as exalted as being faithful to God.

~ Believe

~ God and Angels ~

Existence of God

Believe in the existence of God,
the logical conclusion of a searching mind.

Believe in the existence of God,
the clear sense of a pure soul.

Believe in the existence of God,
the simple acknowledgment of a contrite heart.

Believe in the existence of God,
the common sense of a sincere person.

Believe in the existence of God,
the natural inclination of humankind.

~ Believe

Knowing the Existence of God

Believe that the existence of God can be known,
by anyone who cares to know the truth.

Believe that the existence of God can be known readily,
by anyone who cares to open their mind and heart.

Believe that the existence of God can be known simply,
by anyone who cares to simply know.

Believe that the existence of God can be known with demon-
    strable proof,
by anyone who cares to use their reason and logic.

Believe that the existence of God will be made known to all,
for it is the nature of God to be revealed and made known.

~ Believe

God the Supreme Being

Believe in God, the Ultimate Reality –
the greatest reality of all that is real.

Believe in God, the Almighty Power –
the most powerful of all possessing power.

Believe in God, the Highest Intelligence –
the first word of truth and the last.

Believe in God, the Supreme Being –
the perfection of essence and existence.

Believe in God, a reality and a mystery –
ultimate, almighty, highest, and supreme.

~Believe

Trinity God

Believe in the Father –
the first Name of God, pure Spirit, eternal Being.

Believe in the Son –
the Word of God, made flesh, Jesus the Christ.

Believe in the Holy Spirit –
the Life of God, the spirit of truth, the flame of love.

Believe in the Trinity –
three Divine Persons in One God.

Believe in God –
Who is Trinity, Father, Son, and Holy Spirit.

~ Believe

Jesus Christ

Believe in Jesus of Nazareth,
a true figure and fact in history.

Believe in Jesus, the Word Incarnate,
the Eternal Word taking on flesh, becoming man.

Believe in Jesus, son of Mary and Joseph,
a real person, crucified on a hill.

Believe in Jesus the Christ,
true God and true man, human and divine.

Believe in Jesus Christ,
and accept Him as your personal Lord and Savior.

~ Believe

Jesus, the Way the Truth and the Life

Believe in the Way –
without the Way, there is no real going.

Believe in the Truth –
without the Truth, there is no real knowing.

Believe in the Life –
without the Life, there is no real living.

Believe in Jesus –
Who is the Way, the Truth, and the Life.

Believe in Jesus Christ –
follow the Way, know the Truth, and live the Life!

~ Believe

The Holy Spirit

Believe in the Holy Spirit –
the Spirit inflaming in us the fire of love.

Believe in the Holy Spirit –
the Spirit guiding us to all truth.

Believe in the Holy Spirit –
the Spirit empowering us with the power of God.

Believe in the Holy Spirit –
Who gives us spiritual gifts and fruits to enjoy.

Believe in the Gifts and Fruits of the Holy Spirit,
available for the asking and receiving.

~ Believe

Angels

Believe in the benevolent celestial beings,
intermediaries and messengers between heaven and earth.

Believe in the seraphim, cherubim, thrones, and dominions,
singing the praises and glory of God in the highest.

Believe in the virtues, powers, principalities, archangels,
    and angels,
giving glory and praise to God forever.

Believe in the nine orders of angels,
forming the glorious choir of angels on high.

Believe in your own personal guardian angel,
who guides, protects, and watches over you.

~ Believe

The Devil

Believe in the existence of the devil –
Lucifer the light, and the proud fallen angel.

Believe in the existence of Satan –
who consciously chose not to serve God.

Believe in the existence of other evil spirits –
together they seek the ruin of souls and lives.

Believe in the existence of the great evil one –
his first lie to people is that he doesn't exist.

Believe in the existence of the devil and evil –
be vigilant and always on your guard!

~ Believe

~ Things of God ~

God First

Believe in living for God first –
"I am the Lord your God and I tolerate no rivals."

Believe in doing good for others second –
"Love your neighbor as you love yourself."

Believe in taking care of yourself third –
this is the safe bet if you want to come out ahead.

Believe in the outcome in the race of life –
with God to win, others to place, and yourself to show.

Believe in that order and you will always come out a winner –
it's not a bet; it's a guarantee.

~ Believe

Necessity of God

Believe in the existence of God –
we cannot have existence without God.

Believe in the power of God –
we cannot have abilities without God.

Believe in the grace of God –
we cannot have divine life without God.

Believe in the mercy of God –
we cannot have redemption without God.

Believe in the glory of God –
we cannot have the glory reserved for God alone.

~ Believe

God's Invitation

Believe in God's invitation to faith,
and accept with all your will.

Believe in God's invitation to truth,
and respond with all your mind.

Believe in God's invitation to hope,
and hold with all your might.

Believe in God's invitation to love,
and embrace with all your heart.

Believe in God's invitation to life,
and reply with a resounding yes!

~ Believe

Our God

Believe in our powerful God,
whose power creates the universe in an instant.

Believe in our merciful God,
whose mercy forgives the repentant sinner.

Believe in our knowing God,
whose thought gives us the first and last word of truth.

Believe in our loving God,
whose love converts the hardened of heart.

Believe in our God,
Who is all powerful, all merciful, all knowing, and all loving.

~ Believe

Our Awesome God

Believe that a relationship with God,
is always present as an invitation and a choice.

Believe that the love of God,
is always and unconditionally available to us.

Believe that the will of God,
will never lead us where the grace of God cannot keep us.

Believe that the mercy of God,
is always willing to forgive and ready to redeem.

Believe that a life with God,
is always a possibility waiting to happen.

~ Believe

God's Work in the World

Believe that a perfect God,
works in and through sinful human beings.

Believe that a perfect God,
calls imperfect human beings to do His work in the world.

Believe that our voices and ears are the instruments,
through which God speaks and listens to his children.

Believe that our hands and feet are the tools,
with which God administers to his people.

Believe that our hearts are the means,
by which God spreads His love throughout the world.

~ Believe

Fullness in God

Believe in love and in its desiring –
only in God is love fully experienced.

Believe in truth and in its searching –
only in God is truth fully discovered.

Believe in good and in its application –
only in God is good fully manifested.

Believe in faith and in its practice –
only in God is faith fully lived.

Believe in hope and in its promises –
only in God is hope fully realized.

~ Believe

God's Will

Believe in God's will for you –
it is the very best thing.

Believe in God's will for you –
it is the greatest good possible.

Believe in God's will for you –
it comes from an all knowing God.

Believe in God's will for you –
it comes from an all loving God.

Believe in God's will for you –
there is nothing possible that could be better.

~ Believe

Glory to God

Believe in acknowledging God,
as the cause and reason for your existence.

Believe in thanking God,
for your life and your ability to function.

Believe in offering to God,
your good deeds, sacrifices, and actions.

Believe in giving to God,
praise, honor, and glory befitting God alone.

Believe in doing everything for the greater glory of God,
in time and in eternity.

~ Believe

God's Option for the Poor and Vulnerable

Believe in helping the poor and vulnerable –
they are our brothers and sisters in need.

Believe in solidarity with the poor and vulnerable –
we are called to be our brothers and sisters keepers.

Believe in justice for the poor and vulnerable –
we are called to help them get what they need and deserve.

Believe in special treatment for the poor and vulnerable –
justice implies that special needs require special action.

Believe in a preferential option for the poor and vulnerable –
Jesus has a special place in his heart for them.

~ Believe

The Revealing God

Believe that God only seems to be hidden,
for it is the nature of God to reveal Himself to His creatures.

Believe that we can know of God,
through the beauty and grandeur of creation.

Believe that we can know of God,
through the order in nature and laws that govern the universe.

Believe that we can know of God,
through the love of God shinning through others.

Believe that we can know of God,
through our conscience and God's quiet voice within.

~ Believe

God's Lights

Believe that there is great darkness in the world,
the darkness of falsehood, immorality, idolatry, and despair.

Believe that the darkness of falsehood and lies,
can be overcome by the immense light of Truth.

Believe that the darkness of immorality and hate,
can be overcome by the intense light of Love.

Believe that the darkness of idolatry and apostasy,
can be overcome by the guiding light of Faith.

Believe that the darkness of despair and depression,
can be overcome by the bright light of Hope.

~ Believe

Affinity and God's Purpose

Believe that the stomach was made for food,
and food intended for the stomach.

Believe that the human intellect was made for truth,
and truth intended for the intellect.

Believe that the human heart was made for love,
and love intended for the heart.

Believe that the human person was made for God,
and therein lies the answer to the purpose of life.

Believe that all things were made for a reason and a purpose,
with a God-intended affinity, connection, and relationship.

~ Believe

God's Commandments

Believe that the Ten Commandments come directly from God –
"…listen to what the Lord your God demands of you…"

Believe that the Commandments are clear commands –
"Worship the Lord and do all that He commands."

Believe that the Commandments tell us what we are to do –
"Love Him, serve Him with all your heart, and obey all
    His laws."

Believe that whatever God tells us is for our well being –
"I am giving them to you today for your benefit."

Believe that Moses' final words contain a truth for us all –
"These teachings are not empty words; they are your
    very life."

~ Believe

Ways of God

Believe in a Divine plan,
for with God there is no mere chance.

Believe in the Lord's blessing,
for with God there is no simple luck.

Believe in God-incidence,
for with God there is no mere coincidence.

Believe in Divine Providence,
for with God there is no mysterious synchronicity.

Believe in Supernatural destiny,
for with God there is no blind fate.

~ Believe

~ Spiritual Things ~

Things of the Spirit

Believe in sacred places and spaces –
it is where the physical joins the spiritual.

Believe in the real existence of angels –
they are messengers to help, guide, and protect.

Believe in the afterlife and continued existence –
it is the next and final place.

Believe in eternity and living forever –
this temporal life is but a moment in eternity.

Believe in the spirit and the spiritual –
they are part of our very nature.

~ Believe

Afterlife

Believe that you will die one day –
nobody can escape this inevitable fact of life.

Believe that you will pass to another state of life –
for the immortal human soul will never die.

Believe that you will receive judgment upon your life –
based on your choices and the good you have or haven't done.

*Believe that you will receive your just consequence, for better
    or for worse –*
from God who is both perfect and perfectly just.

*Believe that heaven and hell are definite realities and
    possibilities –*
eternal happiness or eternal suffering.

~ Believe

Eternity

Believe that numbers go on to infinity,
on forever, without a final number and end.

Believe that time goes on to infinity,
now and forever, without a final minute or hour.

Believe that humans are born into eternity,
conceived in time but made to exist forever.

Believe that eternity is something to take very seriously,
for there is no turning back or changing the nature of
    existence.

Believe that God is eternal,
and the goal of life is to be with God for eternity.

~ Believe

Heaven

Believe in perfection,
even though nothing is perfect in this world and life.

Believe in perfect existence,
where there is perfect love, truth, and good.

Believe in a perfect state,
where there is perfect peace, joy, and happiness.

Believe in perfect relationships,
with God, angels, and others.

Believe in heaven, perfection beyond this earthy realm,
the desire of all, the promise of Christ, and the goal of life.

~ Believe

Sin

Believe that sin is something real, a human failing,
that flows from flawed and fallen human nature.

Believe that original sin is the sin we all inherit,
from our first parents, inclining us to sin and evil.

Believe that actual sin is the sin we commit ourselves,
in our free, knowledgeable, and deliberate bad choices.

Believe that sin is turning away from God,
breaking His laws and commandments and disobeying
   His will.

Believe that sin is a moral evil, a refusal to love God
   and others,
and a rejection of the good we ought to do.

~ Believe

The Seven Deadly Sins

Believe that the seven capital vices are opposed to virtue,
and work against the growth of virtue within our soul.

Believe that pride, envy, anger, and sloth,
can be overcome by humility, love, kindness, and zeal.

Believe that greed, gluttony, and lust,
can be overcome by generosity, temperance, and self-control.

Believe that the seven very serious sins,
can cloud our conscience and weaken our wills and judgment.

Believe that the seven deadly sins,
can be deadly to the life of God and the spirit within us.

~ Believe

Sin, Suffering, and Death

Believe that sin is a reality and condition –
part of our fallen human nature and inheritance.

Believe that suffering is not to be avoided at all cost –
rather something to accept and offer up to God.

Believe that death is not meant to be feared –
rather something to acknowledge and prepare for.

Believe that sin, suffering, and death are human realities –
so also are the goodness of human nature, joy, and life.

Believe that human sin, suffering, and death –
can all be overcome through Jesus Christ.

~ Believe

Critical Distinctions

Believe that God is not an impersonal force,
but a personal Being with intelligence and will.

Believe that Jesus Christ is not some great prophet,
rather He is Lord and Savior of the world.

Believe that salvation is achieved not only through
    human effort,
but through collaboration between God and each individual.

Believe that prayer is not a spiritual activity just with oneself,
but conversation, communication, and connection with God.

Believe that the future and destiny is not fixed,
but rather something to freely and actively create.

~ Believe

The Bible

Believe that the Bible is the true Voice of God –
God's revelation to the world.

Believe that the Bible contains the inspired Word of God –
commandments and guidance for life and living.

Believe that the Bible gives us the Truth of God –
God is Truth and His words are true.

Believe that the Holy Spirit, the Paraclete –
is with us and leads us to all truth.

Believe that we learn from Jesus in the Bible –
we read His words, hear His voice, and see His actions.

~ Believe

Miracles

Believe in miracles – something that happens beyond nature,
due to the power of God.

Believe in miracles – an event or occurrence,
meant to help us, bring good, and increase faith.

Believe in miracles – the clear hand of God,
with a point or message for all to heed.

Believe in miracles – a divine gesture,
from God who cares about His people.

Believe in miracles – a gift to us,
from God with love.

~ Believe

Project Sainthood

Believe that most people do not embrace the ideal of sainthood,
because they think it is unattainable for them.

Believe that people find the way of holiness very demanding,
the bar perceived to be set too high and out of reach.

Believe that we cannot take shortcuts and lower the standard,
but we can lessen the distance between the floor and the bar.

Believe that we can shorten the distance and thus the leap,
by stepping up on a stool or ladder before jumping.

Believe that the biggest stool and tallest ladder,
are the blessing, grace, and power of God.

~ Believe

Saints

Believe in the saints in heaven –
the real heroes and heroines of God.

Believe in the holy souls who went before us –
they are our models and inspiration.

Believe in saintly people living today –
take their example and learn from them.

Believe in holy people in your community –
and be positive and optimistic in your own spiritual growth.

Believe in the universal call to holiness –
and embark on the path to personal sanctity.

~ Believe

Saving Your Soul

Believe that you are body and soul, spirit and matter –
and your soul is immaterial and immortal.

Believe that your soul will never cease to exist –
made by God to be with God forever.

Believe that God will judge you when you die –
either to be with God or separated from God for eternity.

*Believe that the overall effort of your entire life must be to
    save your soul –*
in the end, absolutely nothing else matters.

Believe that saving your immortal soul –
is your most important concern and greatest task in this life!

~ Believe

~ Additional Important Things ~

The Five Most Important Things to Believe In

Believe in God, the true and living God of us all,
for all and everything else flows from this first truth.

Believe in the fundamental goodness of all God's creation,
the universe and all living things, especially humans.

Believe in the universal call to know the true and do the good,
and to live the theological virtues of faith, hope, and love.

Believe in loving God with all your heart, soul, mind,
    and body,
and love your neighbor as you would love yourself.

Believe in being redeemed by Jesus Christ and saving
    your soul,
thus enjoying perfect and eternal happiness in heaven
    with God.

~ *Believe*

The Purpose of Life

Believe that the purpose of life is threefold in nature,
concerning our knowing, our doing, and our attaining.

Believe that the purpose of life is to know God,
for God made us specifically with the intention to know Him.

Believe that the purpose of life is to love God,
for God made us to love us and we to love Him.

Believe that the purpose of life is to attain heaven,
for God made us to be with Him forever in His presence.

Believe that the purpose of life is to know and love God
  in this life,
and attain heaven and be with God forever in the next life.

~ Believe

Life's Paradoxes

Believe in the intellectual paradox of truth –
where the subjective and objective meet and cross over.

Believe in the paradox of God's Word –
believing leads to knowing; through belief we know.

Believe in the beautiful paradox of love –
love has no reason; love loves because it loves.

Believe in the paradox of the Christian life –
he who loses his life will gain it.

Believe in the truths contained within paradoxes –
the contradictions are only apparent, not actual.

~ Believe

Fundamental Paradigms

Believe that a paradigm is a belief system and conceptual framework,
a way to understand reality, and make sense of things.

Believe that there are only two fundamental paradigms,
with all paradigms falling into one or the other.

Believe that one paradigm revolves around God,
where God is the measure and judge of all things.

Believe that the other paradigm revolves around humans,
where man is the measure and judge of all things.

Believe that the paradigm we adopt determines all,
so rightfully acknowledge God; otherwise would be
utter folly.

~ Believe

From Believing to Knowing

Believe that believing is the simple and common way,
for people to connect to what is objectively true and good.

Believe that in believing, one believes something to be true,
whereas in knowing, one knows something to be true.

Believe that the act of believing is like stepping out,
and living the content of what we believe is true.

Believe that in living the content of what we believe true,
we can begin to experience its actual truth and goodness.

Believe that in experiencing its truth and goodness,
we now know as true what we once believed was true.

~ Believe

The Great Errors

Believe that there are two grave errors of our time –
found in the intellectual and moral orders.

Believe that something is not true because I believe it so –
rather I believe it so because I think it is true.

"It's not true because I say it. I say it because it's true."

Believe that something is not good because I believe it so –
rather I believe it so because I think it is good.

"It's not good because I say it. I say it because it's good."

Believe that true and good, truth and goodness –
adhere in things independently of human minds and beliefs.

Believe that the Greeks had a name for people who
    didn't see this –
the word was *dementia* and many are those who suffer
    from it today.

~ Believe

Matter and Form

Believe that all that is, all that exists, is being,
and all beings have matter and form, except for God, angels,
    and demons.

Believe that natural created beings have matter and form,
a distinction in the mind but always one in reality.

Believe that primary matter is the physical,
whereas form is that which makes something to be what it is.

Believe that with human beings, a body and soul composite,
the body is the matter and the soul is the form.

Believe everything has a material and formal consideration,
and we cannot ignore the consequences and ramifications.

~ Believe

Essence and Existence

Believe that every real being has essence and existence –
every real being is something and every real being exists.

The question "whether" something is, is one thing –
the question "what" something is, is another.

The questions of essence and existence remain distinct –
with all created beings in existence in the world.

With God who is eternal and not a created being –
His essence is to exist; essence and existence are one.

We should not be surprised when Moses asked God
    who He was –
and God replied, "I am who I am… This is my name forever."

~ Believe

Being and Doing

Believe that the distinction between being and doing,
applied to human beings is most critical and crucial.

Believe that being has to do with what we are in our nature,
whereas doing has to do with our actions and behavior.

Believe that in our being humans are entirely good,
whereas in our doing, we are good or bad, virtuous or vicious.

Believe that humans are sinful in thought and action,
but we remain fundamentally good in our human nature.

Believe that we should celebrate our goodness and worth,
while always striving to overcome our imperfect actions.

~ Believe

Knowing and Loving

Believe that the great two powers of the human soul,
are intellect and free will.

Believe that knowing pertains to the intellect,
and loving pertains to the will.

Believe that much knowing makes us a genius,
while much loving makes us a saint.

Believe that in the end God judges us,
according to how loving we are, not how smart.

Believe that knowledge can help us to love more,
while love can help us to gain more knowledge.

~ Believe

The World, the Devil, and the Flesh

Believe that the three main things that detract us from God,
are the world, the devil, and the flesh.

Believe that the world offers so many distractions,
goods, pleasures, and busy things to occupy us.

Believe that the devil is always trying to tempt us,
with ways and things that are not of God and love.

Believe that our own material and carnal desires,
in excess or disordered can lead us away from God.

Believe that we are in the world but not of it,
and the devil must be resisted and our desires properly
    ordered.

~ Believe

The Great Misconception

I believe one of the greatest misconceptions in the minds of people today has to do with the common misunderstanding of the phrase, "believing in God." The phrase, "believing in God," was never meant to be equated with whether or not one believes in the existence of God. The phrase "believing in God" is meant to be understood as, "Do you believe in what God has said? Do you believe in the Ten Commandments, which God has given to us? Do you believe in the teachings of Jesus, which are contained in Scripture? Believing in what God has said and revealed involves a specific response to specific words, teaching, directives, etc. Put more simply, the question ought to read, "Do you believe God?" This is the same as asking, "Do you believe your friend? Do you believe your teacher? Do you believe the bus driver? This understanding presupposes that something was actually said and so believing is a real response to a real person, be it friend, teacher, bus driver, or God.

Most people will equate this phrase, "believing in God," with believing in the existence of God. Hence, the question, "Do you believe in the existence of God?" One answers, "Yes, I believe," and believes, acts, and lives accordingly. This act of believing opens the door to specific beliefs, practices, and lifestyle, based on what one believes God is saying and means. Very good. One answers, "No, I do not believe," and believes, acts, and lives accordingly. This act of disbelieving closes the door to anything based on what God says or means. Very easy and convenient. One has just closed the door in God's face, and dismissed God in one smooth and seemingly justifiable short statement. The person usually does not feel any discomfort, guilt, or remorse, because "people have a right to believe in anything they want." The person chooses not to believe in God and therefore God or the idea of God has no relevance for them, or so they think.

To not believe in what God has said is pure and absolute folly and an outright rejection of God. It really amounts to intellectual and moral suicide. God by nature is omniscient and is all knowing, not to mention all loving as well. Whatever God says is true, God who can neither deceive nor be deceived. Who are we to argue with God or question the mind of God? Are our minds and judgments greater than God's? Of course not! But this has been the temptation of man since the beginning of time. We hear it and see it all around us – "I will not serve!" The brightest of the angels succumbed to this great temptation. We should not be surprised that many a human has fallen also. God has indeed spoken and let us not be convinced otherwise. God invites our positive response in an act of believing. Open your heart with love and accept all that God reveals and open your mind like a sponge and soak up all the truth God shares and showers us with us.

The Five Most Important Questions in Life

Who and what are you? I am a human being, body and soul, made in the image and likeness of **God**. I possess the powers of intellect and free will. I enjoy inherent goodness, value, worth, and dignity. I have my own unique identity, character, personality, and essence. I have a name. I am loveable.

What do you believe and know? I know that **God** exists and I believe all that **God** reveals to me. I believe in goodness, truth, and beauty. I believe and know the truth of many things and I believe in the goodness and value of many things. I know I am incomplete in my nature and I desire happiness and fulfillment.

What do you do? I exist, live, breathe, and move. I try to live a life of faith, hope, and love. I value people and I foster good relationships. I have a job and I work. I help others. I try to keep fit and healthy. I strive to know and love **God** continually and I strive for wellness, wholeness, happiness, and holiness.

Where did you come from? I came from **God**. **God** created my soul out of nothing and my parents supplied the matter which was conjoined with my soul at conception. I was conceived in time and place, from non-existence to existence. Before I existed, I was a thought in the mind of **God** and a desire of my parents.

Where are you going? I am going to **God**. I am going to heaven to be with **God** for eternity. All activities, events, goals, places, and destinations are partial and temporary, all tributaries flowing to my ultimate and final destination. Every step I take in this life is a step on the road to heaven.

"It's good to wonder, reflect and be a thinker but sooner or later you must believe and be a believer. And in so doing, the world will open itself up to you – its truth, its goodness, and its beauty. Close your eyes and you will begin to truly see God and the things of the spirit. Be inspired and be motivated – embrace life and be happy."

~ Author

Essential Believing

~ Believe in God... even when you don't sense the Divine.

~ Believe in love... even when you don't feel it.

~ Believe in friendship... even when it has been betrayed.

~ Believe in trust... even when it has been broken.

~ Believe in truth... even when you don't grasp it.

~ Believe in hope... even when all appears lost.

~ Believe in peace... even when there is turmoil all around.

~ Believe in joy... even when there is sadness and despair.

~ Believe in others... even when they fail you.

~ Believe in better days... even when the present is difficult and painful.

~ Believe in the Christmas Spirit... even when others don't believe.

~ Believe in your goodness, worth, and dignity... even when others treat you otherwise.

~ Believe in yourself... even when you feel down and out.

~ Believe in victory... even when the struggle seems endless.

~ Believe in your dreams... even when others don't support you.

~ Believe in family... even when it is imperfect or broken.

~ Believe in respect... even when it is not given.

~ Believe in change... even when you are not growing and feel stuck.

~ Believe in your inner power and strength... even when you feel weak and vulnerable.

~ Believe in good... even when you witness evil.

~ Believe in prayer... even when you don't yet see results.

~ Believe in ideals... even when they seem distant and beyond reach.

~ Believe in laughter... even when all you want to do is cry.

~ Believe in higher and better... even when you lack energy and motivation.

~ Believe in living... even when there doesn't seem to be any point.

~ Believe in happiness... even when you are unhappy and sad.

~ Believe in personal transformation... even when the hurdles appear insurmountable.

~ Believe in freedom... even when you are confined or oppressed.

~ Believe in success... even when you have failed.

~ Believe in the future... even when the past has been hard and the present difficult.

~ Believe in the light... even when the darkness envelopes you.

~ Believe in health... even when you are tired of being sick.

~ Believe in vision... even when your eyes are closed.

~ Believe in vitality... even when you are tired and depressed.

~ Believe in enlightenment... even though ignorance abounds.

~ Believe in justice... even when injustice has occurred.

~ Believe in beauty... even when it has been obscured or masked.

~ Believe in spiritual things... even when material things prevail.

~ Believe in miracles... even when you haven't experienced one yet.

~ Believe in the rainbow... even when you're in the storm.

~ Believe in life having a purpose... even though you question your existence.

~ Believe in meaning... even when you can't seem to make any sense.

~ Believe in fulfillment... even when you don't see your potential.

~ Believe in your personal destiny... even when you don't see any plan.

~ Believe in your abilities... even when your accomplishments are few.

~ Believe in right... even when you're not sure what *is* right.

~ Believe in second chances... even when you feel you're undeserving.

~ Believe in your child... even when he or she has gone wayward.

~ Believe in the afterlife... even though it is shrouded in mystery.

~ Believe in your parents... even though they make mistakes.

~ Believe in risk... even when you are afraid.

~ Believe in angels... even though you can't see them.

~ Believe in commitment... even when it has been broken.

~ Believe in healing... even when the cut is deep and the wound is open.

~ Believe in virtue... even though vice can be attractive.

~ Believe in gifts... even though at times they are not freely given.

~ Believe in high standards... even though they require much work to achieve.

~ Believe in order and unity... even though there is chaos and disorder in life.

~ Believe in the color of life... even when there are dreary grays of human existence.

~ Believe in that special someone... even though there are many possible ones.

~ Believe in your personal story... even when others don't listen to it.

~ Believe in your own importance... even when others don't acknowledge it.

~ Believe in a smile... even when others don't smile at you.

~ Believe in your uniqueness... even though you share the same human nature.

~ Believe in values... even when things are not valued.

~ Believe in principles... even when they are not adhered to.

~ Believe in your inner core... even when you feel your very being fading away.

~ Believe in your own ideas and aspirations... even when others ridicule you.

~ Believe in companionship... even when you are lonely.

~ Believe in winning... even when you have lost.

~ Believe in optimism... even when surrounded by pessimism.

~ Believe in being positive... even though it's easier to be negative.

~ Believe in self-confidence... even when you are not feeling it.

~ Believe in your destination... even though you are not there yet.

~ Believe in character... even though many people are superficial and shallow.

~ Believe in selflessness... even though selfishness is commonplace.

~ Believe in the sacred... even when you are caught up in the human.

~ Believe in people... even when they are ignorant or mean.

~ Believe in the small things... even when they don't seem to make a difference.

~ Believe in sacrifice... even though it is difficult.

~ Believe in holiness... even though it may seem unattainable.

~ Believe in improvement... even when it seems impossible.

~ Believe in your personal gifts... even when they are not yet developed.

~ Believe in relationships .... even when some break up and end.

~ Believe in wisdom... even though it is a rare commodity.

~ Believe in knowledge... even though it takes work and discipline.

~ Believe in understanding... even though it takes an extra effort.

~ Believe in your destiny... even though it is not clear.

~ Believe in laughter... even when there are tears.

~ Believe in fun... even when sometimes we have to make the effort.

~ Believe in self-esteem... even when you are feeling low.

~ Believe in self-reliance... even when you need to rely on others.

~ Believe in self-worth... even when others de-value you.

~ Believe in your capabilities... even when you feel incapable.

~ Believe in taking a chance... even though it is easier to do the safe thing.

~ Believe in stepping out in faith... even though there is no footing in sight.

~ Believe in surprise... even when people think you are silly.

~ Believe in humor... even when others don't laugh.

~ Believe in acceptance... even though it can be very difficult.

~ Believe in openness... even though it takes patience.

~ Believe in challenge... even when the going is steep and difficult.

~ Believe in quest... even though it takes resolve and determination.

~ Believe in mission... even though it takes perseverance and effort.

~ Believe in task... even though it takes hard work.

~ Believe in calling... even when you just want to do your own thing.

~ Believe in reality... even when you feel you are losing touch with it.

~ Believe in intuition... even when your mind is not certain.

~ Believe in gut feeling... even when there is no logical explanation.

~ Believe in opportunity... even when you cannot see any.

~ Believe in passion... even when you lack energy, drive, and feeling.

~ Believe in love... even when there is indifference and hatred.

~ Believe in truth... even though many people are skeptical.

~ Believe in faith... even though doubt often seems more common.

~ Believe in hope... even when you can't see what you hope for.

~ Believe in goodness... even though many people don't really care.

~ Believe in reconciliation... even though it is difficult to forgive.

~ Believe in wholeness... even when things are fragmented.

~ Believe in healing... even when there is broken-ness.

~ Believe in roots... even though you sometimes feel uprooted and alienated.

~ Believe in heaven... even though it is beyond this earthly realm.

~ Believe in yourself... even when nobody else seems to believe in you.

~ Believe in journey... even though it begins with the single step.

~ Believe in adventure... even though there is no telling where it will all lead.

~ Believe in eternity... even though it is a difficult concept to grasp.

~ Believe in Jesus... the Christ, God and man, human and divine.

~ Believe in the Holy Spirit... the Spirit of God, the breath of Life and Love.

~ Believe in the Father... who together with Son and Spirit are Trinity.

~ Believe in God... the alpha and the omega, the beginning and the end.

~ Believe in everything important in life!

"The greatest thing human is not constructing tall buildings, winning gold medals, or accumulating material wealth, but in loving others and being loved in return. It is also the most beautiful thing."

~ Author

~ Special Addition~

The Human Heart and the Many Faces of Love

Introduction

L ove. There is perhaps no other word that will elicit such
an interest and response in the minds and hearts of
people universally as the word love. The idea of love has been
most fertile, giving birth to a continuous stream of writing by
poets, philosophers, theologians, psychologists, novelists, and
the like. Love is held up as the highest of values – "and the
greatest of these is love." The deepest longing of the human
heart is said to be love, the reaching out to fulfill that which
yearns to be filled. The greatest desires are the desires of love.
The greatest passions are passions inflamed with love. The
greatest thing in this life, it is said, is to love another and to be
loved in return. People have lived and died for love. Love of
God has inspired countless men and women to give of themselves and their lives in service to others. Love can give us
heart pounding romance, deep and lasting friendships, authentic affirmation of our being, nurturing of our developing
selves, and much, much more.

The longer we live, the more kinds of love we experience
and the meaning of love broadens and deepens. Love is something we can all readily relate to but it is also something which
can cause much confusion and turmoil. We all know and
understand something of love but there remains the misunder-
standings and the mystery. Questions are asked: "What is love?
How can I experience love? How can I be more loving? Who

and where is the love of my life? How can I stay in love?" The quest for the experience and understanding of love is one of the fundamental quests of life. The quest for love is a quest of all of us, springing from the well and desire of human nature. My quest for love and your personal quest for love are part of the shared and fundamental quest for love of the whole human race. Our individual quests for love do not remain an isolated blip on the horizon or as a bold character going it alone. We join with all of humankind in the universal quest for love. We are all individuals and take a different path on the journey of life, experience our unique adventure, encounter different challenges, and create our own personal odyssey, but the fundamental human quests presented to us in life are the same.

The last several years have been for me a very active time in my insight and understanding of love. Through experience, thought, reflection, observation, reading, discussion, sharing and prayer, I feel I have gained a very interesting and unique perspective on the nature of love. I also feel compelled to share with you what I have found. In my odyssey and quest for love, I imagine myself beginning the descent down from a mountain. I have been up and down several mountains, through numerous valleys, over countless hills, across endless plains and hot, barren deserts. I have traversed frigid wastelands, escaped danger in dense jungles, swam across raging rivers, fallen into quick sand, and fortunately rescued by angels in street clothes.

What I desire to share with you is by no means exhaustive, for the topic and subject of love is extremely rich and fertile. I hope that my small and unique work on love will help others understand love better, prompt and help us all to love more in practice. One of the enduring questions of life is "What is love?" With a practical approach and perspective, I offer over two hundred snapshots or "faces of love." I also share snap-shots of pseudo or false love, as I perceive them to be. I hope you get as interested and excited in reading "The Human Heart and the Many Faces of Love," as I did in reflecting upon and writing them. Believe in love!

The Many Faces of Love

From the heart – spoken and unspoken, whispered and in silence, what we mean or possibly mean when we say, "I love you." Intentions, sentiments and acts of love emanating from the human heart, mostly for the better and sometimes for worse, the following are over two hundred "faces" of love of the human experience, in the concrete and particular moments of our daily lives. The idea and reality of love is immensely rich and fertile.

1. **Affection** – "I love you," meaning I have affection for you. I feel affectionate towards you. I have good, positive, and warm feelings toward you. I feel good and content in your presence.

2. **Affirmation** – "I love you," meaning I affirm you. In your person and being, I acknowledge and affirm your goodness, value, worth, and dignity as a unique individual and as a human being.

3. **Desire** – "I love you," meaning I desire you. You are the object of my desire. You appeal to me and I am attracted to you. I sense myself gravitating toward you and I want to be with you.

4. **Nurture** – "I love you," meaning I nurture and care for you. I take care of you, attend to your basic needs, and help you to grow and develop into a happy, secure, and self-confident person.

5. **Dependency** – "I love you," meaning I am dependent upon you. I need you to care, guide, model, teach, and help me, in my lack and limitedness, as I grow and develop toward fulfillment.

6. **Love of God** – "I love you," meaning I humble myself and bow before you my God. I am open to your love and will for me. I adore and worship you. I obey your commandments and law.

7. **Friendship** – "I love you," meaning I value and appreciate you. I value our bond, mutual interests, sharing, and supporting and affirming each other. I desire your good and happiness.

8. **Unconditional** – "I love you," meaning I love and have love for you unconditionally. There are no reasons, conditions or requirements set upon you. I love you simply because I love.

9. **Infatuation** – "I love you," meaning I enjoy my great feelings of love for you. I love all the excitement and positive feelings I have because of you. I am caught up in my own feelings.

10. **Parental** – "I love you," meaning I treasure you. You are special to me. I take pride in being your parent. I acknowledge the physical and spiritual bond between us. We are forever tied.

11. **Child** – "I love you," meaning I am me because of you. I am somebody. I feel safe and secure. I am happy to know my roots and all that you give and do for me. I have identity.

12. **Intimacy** – "I love you," meaning I feel and sense you in our closeness at a deep level. I enjoy and value our closeness and intimacy. I begin to really see and hear you.

13. **Union** – "I love you," meaning I experience you in our oneness. Our intimacy leads to this deeper and beautiful relationship as we strive to be closer and more as one in love.

14. **Sibling** – "I love you," meaning I value and appreciate you in the blood bond between us. I am fortunate to have you as brother or sister. You and our childhood memories are special to me.

15. **Trust** – "I love you," meaning I believe and trust you. I am stepping out on a limb in good faith, believing in you and what you say. I am taking a risk, making myself vulnerable.

16. **Respect** – "I love you," meaning I respect you. I hold you in basic human esteem and worth and extend to you basic dignity, in virtue of the simple fact that you are a human being.

17. **Commitment** – "I love you," meaning I make a commitment to you. I freely make a choice and decision to commit myself to you in relationship. I am investing myself and my time in you.

18. **Enjoyment** – "I love you," meaning I like and enjoy the experiences I have with you. I enjoy your company and your conversation. I appreciate and value the enjoyment with you.

19. **Faithfulness** – "I love you," meaning I resolve to be faithful to you. I will be loyal, devoted and true. I will uphold my promises and commitment to you. You can count on me.

20. **Being** – "I love you," meaning I give myself to you. I give you my being – who and what I am. I don't do for you. I am for you. I don't give you things. I give you myself. Being is the core of who I am.

21. **Special Bond** – "I love you," meaning I appreciate and thank you for being you. You are very special to me. You have touched my life and me in some positive and significant way.

22. **Mystical** – "I love you," meaning I experience God. I feel the love, power, and mystery of God in a direct, unhindered way. God is communicating to me quietly, surely and peacefully.

23. **Human Kind** – "I love you," meaning I feel care and concern for all people. I have good feelings for the entire human race. We are all brothers and sisters on our shared planet.

24. **Gender** – "I love you," meaning I like you in your gender. Your femininity is appealing and my masculinity is moved. Your masculinity is appealing and my femininity is moved.

25. **Marriage** – "I love you," meaning I cherish and value you in our marriage relationship. I confirm my commitment and trust in you, and respect for you. We are one couple, one partnership, one team, and one family.

26. **Romantic** – "I love you," meaning I feel romantic towards you. I want to do something special and memorable that acknowledges and celebrates our togetherness and special relationship.

27. **Need** – "I love you," meaning I need and depend on you. I feel positive towards you, because you are fulfilling my unsatisfied needs for security, affirmation, and emotional support.

28. **Fall** – "I love you," meaning I have fallen for you. I find myself with an unexpected attraction with great and wonderful feelings for you. Things have moved very quickly.

29. **Sacrifice** – "I love you," meaning I sacrifice for you. I give up my time, energy and self for your wishes, needs, good, happiness, and fulfillment. I do this freely and willingly.

30. **Obedience** – "I love you," meaning I obey you. I freely, actively, gladly and whole-heartedly do what you positively wish and tell me to do. I trust you and I take your lead and direction.

31. **Admiration** – "I love you," meaning I admire you. I see your great quality of character or greatness of achievement and you show me what I am capable of doing. I am very impressed and you inspire me.

32. **Passion** – "I love you," meaning I have great energy for you. Intense thoughts, feelings, and sensations have been aroused. I want to connect and bond. I feel excited and alive with you!

33. **Thanksgiving** – "I love you," meaning I really thank you. I am so very grateful for what you have done for me. I thank you sincerely from the bottom of my heart.

34. **Relatives** – "I love you," meaning I honor you in our relations. I acknowledge our blood and family tie. I honor the connection we have that is basic and constant, historical and genetic.

35. **Empathy** – "I love you," meaning I empathize with you. I sense and feel what you are going through. I "see" your experience. I have understanding and compassion for you. I feel for you.

36. **Spiritual** – "I love you," meaning I feel and sense a deep unspoken connection between us. Though not in each other's physical presence, you are my friend, advisor, counsel, and comfort.

37. **Forgiveness** – "I love you," meaning I forgive you. I know and acknowledge your offense against me and I am letting go of it from my heart. I harbor no resentment or ill thoughts.

38. **Apology** – "I love you," meaning I apologize. I am sorry for the wrong I have done against you. I feel bad. I feel remorse. I will try not to do it again. I ask for your forgiveness.

39. **Kindred Spirit** – "I love you," meaning I feel a special connection with you. I see you in a special light. You and I are of "like kind" in many different and significant ways.

40. **Soul Mate** – "I love you," meaning you are the special and unique one for me. I sense very strongly and mysteriously we were made for each other. We connect and bond at a deep level.

41. **Surrender** – "I love you," meaning I surrender myself to You, O God. I submit to you. Out of love for You, I willingly and gladly place myself in your service, under your command.

42. **Restraint** – "I love you," meaning I restrain myself. I hold back from saying, doing, or acting, which I could rightfully and truthfully do, but for your good, I refrain from doing so.

43. **Letting Go** – "I love you," meaning I let you be free. I don't try to control or manipulate you. I let you be responsible for your own actions. I allow you to grow and develop.

44. **Service** – "I love you," meaning I serve you. I carry out acts of service, doing good and helping you, responding to your needs. I am not your "slave" – I am willingly at your service.

45. **Freedom** – "I love you," meaning I respect your freedom. Freedom is yours to possess and enjoy. It is part of your nature, a right to exercise responsibly. I allow you self-determination.

46. **Discipline** – "I love you," meaning I discipline myself for you. I control my thoughts and speech. I control my feelings, emotions, passions, and actions for your good and human dignity.

47. **Formative** – "I love you," meaning I form you in your growth and development. I help mold you in your character and other facets of your being, with your true and real good in mind.

48. **Beautiful** – "I love you," meaning I am attracted to your outer appearance. You look beautiful and gorgeous to me. I really like what I see! You excite me and I enjoy looking at you.

49. **Angel** – "I love you," meaning I thank you for being like an angel to me. God has delivered a clear message to me through you. Thank you for being an instrument, a channel, a messenger.

50. **Bubbling** – "I love you," meaning I am overflowing with good thoughts and feelings over you. I am positive, optimistic, cheerful and feeling wonderful! It's just happening.

51. **Mystery** – "I love you," meaning it is difficult to explain my thoughts, feelings, and attraction to you. My mind tries to grapple with the mystery and complexity. I don't understand.

52. **Promise** – "I love you," meaning I hold to my pledge to you. Whatever I have promised to you, I remain faithful, steadfast and true to it and to you. My promise is a decision I make.

53. **Natural** – "I love you," meaning I have much in my heart for you and it is "natural" for me to feel and be this way it seems. You elicit these responses from me, and they flow easily.

54. **Healing** – "I love you," meaning I thank you for your healing touch. I acknowledge the significant healing I have experienced through you. I am indebted to you. Thank you.

55. **Dignity** – "I love you," meaning I uphold your dignity. I see, acknowledge, and respect your innate human dignity. You deserve to be treated this way simply because you are a human being.

56. **Supportive** – "I love you," meaning I support you. In all your endeavors, joys and sorrows, struggles, difficulties, aims, and goals of life, I support you in doing the best thing for yourself.

57. **Care** – "I love you," meaning I care about you. I care about things that mean something to you and have an impact upon you and your life. I care about your well-being and your happiness.

58. **Remorse** – "I love you," meaning I feel remorse for having offended you. In my doing wrong or harm against you, I feel very bad as I am the cause for your undue pain or suffering.

59. **Encouragement** – "I love you," meaning I encourage you. I encourage you to be the best you can be, to have aims and goals in life, to work hard toward those goals and to be happy.

60. **Imprint** – "I love you," meaning our relationship has marked me. You have been imprinted upon me and embedded within me. I will never be the same again. You are part of who I am.

61. **Platonic** – "I love you," meaning I connect and relate to you in a physically limited and emotionally detached way. Our relating is predominantly of the mind, will, and soul.

62. **Altruism** – "I love you," meaning I love you altruistically. I love you with pure intentions, not for my good, or for ulterior motives, but simply and honestly for you alone, for your good.

63. **Making Love** – "I love you," meaning I engage in sexual intercourse with you. This intimacy is an expression and act of love, a giving of body, heart, and self to one another.

64. **Like** – "I love you," meaning I like you. I like so many things about you – your manner, your laugh, your ambition, your interests, your smile, your attitude. I really like you!

65. **For the love of God** – "I love you," meaning I do good for you out of love for God. My love for God moves me to love you, as an overflow of the love of God that is alive within me.

66. **In the love of God** – "I love you," meaning I love you, we love each other, we both love God and God loves us. We are bound together not as two but in the love of God as three.

67. **Martyrdom** – "I love you," meaning I give up my life for You my God. At the threat of death to renounce You and the truth of the faith I hold, I choose and accept death, rather than denial.

68. **Ultimate sacrifice** – "I love you," meaning I give up my life for you. In a life-threatening situation, where one of us will die, I will accept death and allow you to live.

69. **Understanding** – "I love you," meaning I understand you. I desire to know and understand you and my heart sees you and understands you. To know you more is to love you more.

70. **Discretion** – "I love you," meaning I tell you what you need to know. For your good, I don't tell you all that I know. Some things would devastate you or cause you great grief or harm.

71. **Acceptance** – "I love you," meaning I accept you. I accept you completely for who you are as a human being. You are good, worthy, and deserving of respect and dignity as you are.

72. **Love at first sight** – "I love you," meaning the very first time I looked at you, I felt love. I still feel that same love, as well as desire and attraction. My eyes are connected to my heart.

73. **First love** – "I love you," meaning I am experiencing this thing called love for the first time. "It is wonderful and magical! It is beautiful and great! I love her! She loves me!"

74. **Puppy love** – "I love you," meaning I have light and elementary feelings of attraction for you. "He noticed me. He talked to me. She's cute. She smiled at me. I think she likes me."

75. **Disinterested** – "I love you," meaning I am not interested in anyone else except you. I put aside all other love interests and focus on you at this moment and time. You alone have my thoughts and attention.

76. **Undying** – "I love you," meaning I love you now and I will love you throughout my entire life. My love for you will not be extinguished; it will not die. It will only grow and get stronger.

77. **Eternal** – "I love you," meaning I love you now, throughout my entire life and forever into eternity. I believe love endures and can last forever, for all eternity, without end.

78. **Silent** – "I love you," meaning I love you even though I don't say it. My thoughts, feelings, intentions, and actions all speak of love for you. All the little things I do for you I do out of love.

79. **Bliss** – "I love you," meaning I am so happy with you! Everything is so great and wonderful. I don't have a major care or problem to worry about. I really enjoy being with you. Life is wonderful!

80. **Summative** – "I love you," meaning all the varied and different things I do for you and the way I am with you must add up to love! The whole is greater than the sum of the parts.

81. **Choice** – "I love you," meaning I choose you. My act of choosing you among all I could have chosen is an act of love. I chose you and no other. My choice is exclusive and so are you.

82. **Our love** – "I love you," meaning I love you and I love our love. I love the fact that we are in love. Our love is something to be acknowledged, celebrated, and cherished. Here's to our love!

83. **Perfect** – "I love you," meaning in this moment I feel love for you and everything is perfect. There is nothing I lack and nothing more I desire. There is no other place I would rather be.

84. **God is Love** – "I love you," meaning I begin to see and understand that You, O God, are Love. Love is not God but God *is* Love. This profound distinction and equating helps us to understand both God and love.

85. **Acts of love for God** – "I love you," meaning I love God in the many little and ordinary acts throughout the day. Many things can be an act of love with the right intention and disposition.

86. **Secret love** – "I love you," meaning I love you but nobody knows about it. It is a secret. I am your secret admirer. I am too shy or reluctant to tell you or anybody else.

87. **Open** – "I love you," meaning I am open to you. I give you my time and I am open to listen to you, to hear whatever you have to say. I give you room and space to be free to be yourself.

88. **Let be loved** – "I love you," meaning I let you love me. I receive your love and good intentions, words, and actions. I see your love and I welcome it sincerely and warmly.

89. **Pain** – "I love you," meaning I allow pain for your good. I allow you to experience discomfort, pain, and suffering for your good, benefit and growth. Don't be afraid of pain.

90. **I love you** – "I love you," meaning I verbalize the "three golden words" aloud. No explanation is required, planned or necessary and these words, uttered sincerely, go straight to the heart.

91. **Overcoming** – "I love you," meaning I overcome human difficulties and go out to you in love. Despite my natural reservation, I show genuine love for you. God empowers me.

92. **Defend** – "I love you," meaning I defend you. I defend your life, your human dignity, your freedom, your rights, your good name, and your family. I actively come to your defense.

93. **Enable** – "I love you," meaning I enable you. I encourage, help, and enable you to do whatever you need to get done, although I don't want you to become dependent or lazy.

94. **Change** – "I love you," meaning I will change for the better for you. I see my faults and shortcomings and because I love you, I willingly change for you, for me, for us, for good.

95. **Die to self** – "I love you," meaning I die to myself for you. I willingly suspend and give up my needs, wants, and desires, so you can enjoy something or benefit in some way for your good.

96. **Don't count the cost** – "I love you," meaning I love you without thinking about my personal cost. You don't have to pay me back. I love and give freely and unconditionally.

97. **Presence** – "I love you," meaning I am present to you. I am here for you. I focus on you, on your needs, questions and concerns. How are you? What can I do for you? How can I help?

98. **Fight** – "I love you," meaning I fight for you. I fight for your good, for what is right and just. I fight and resist evil in all its guises. I take up arms to fight in self-defense if necessary.

99. **Patience** – "I love you," meaning I am patient with you. My being patient allows you to formulate your thoughts, speak uninterrupted, relax, think, question, react, and respond.

100. **Work** – "I love you," meaning I work for you. The job I undertake, the toil I endure, and the work I complete is for your good in some way. It is a labor of love.

101. **Obligation** – "I love you," meaning I oblige myself to you. The duties and obligations I take on are for your benefit. I don't have to do them. I choose to do them for you.

102. **Pray** – "I love you," meaning I pray for you. I believe in the power of prayer and the fact that God hears my petition for your necessity or good. God will act in some way for you.

103. **Best** – "I love you," meaning I desire and do what is best for you. What is best for you is not necessarily what you want, or what I want. What is best for you stands alone, as objectively good.

104. **Wait** – "I love you," meaning I will wait for you. I love you and I will wait for you to return. You are the one for me and we for each other, and waiting is but a temporary thing.

105. **Indulge** – "I love you," meaning I indulge you in something special or something I know you like. I treat you extra special in a situation or moment. I make an extra effort for you.

106. **Captivated** – "I love you," meaning I am captivated by you. I am held spellbound. You are so interesting to look at and listen to. I am captivated by your unique person and qualities.

107. **Glory to God** – "I love you," meaning the good I do, I do for God, out of love for God, for the greater glory of God, in time and in eternity. The honor and the glory is reserved for God alone.

108. **Fondness** – "I love you," meaning I am very fond of you. We have known each other for a long time; we are comfortable with each other. I respect and trust you; you are nice; I like you.

109. **Teach** – "I love you," meaning I teach you for your good. I teach from the heart desiring you to see and understand the important truths I wish to impart. My teaching is an act of love.

110. **Endure pain** – "I love you," meaning I am enduring pain for your good. At this moment, I am in pain and it is necessary to accept it in order to achieve something truly good for you. It is not easy.

111. **Beauty** – "I love you," meaning I see your beauty. You are so beautiful to me. Your unique combination of outer looks and inner character and disposition is attractive and appealing.

112. **Crush** – "I love you," meaning I have a crush on you. To a certain degree, I am attracted to you and you appeal to me. I find you interesting. I talk about you. I want to go out with you.

113. **Luv you** – "I love you," meaning I really like you. I like you in many ways and I want to express it greater than a simple liking. Luv expresses my feelings very well right now.

114. **Kindness** – "I love you," meaning I am kind to you. I show and extend this to you in many different ways – by being polite, showing consideration, sharing things, listening, and smiling.

115. **Comfort** – "I love you," meaning I comfort you in your discomfort, pain, suffering, or agony. I offer you some relief through my empathy, understanding, presence, and support.

116. **Not envious** – "I love you," meaning I am not envious of what you have. You have good things and I am happy for you. You have achieved great things and I am happy with you.

117. **Listen** – "I love you," meaning I listen to you. I actively tune in and listen to you. I am present, really hear, and listen to what you are saying. I care and try to understand you.

118. **Not possessive** – "I love you," meaning I am not possessive of what I have. My possessions are mine but I don't mind sharing them with you, my friends and those in need.

119. **Believe** – "I love you," meaning I believe in you. I believe in your goodness. I believe in your potential, capabilities and abilities. I believe you can do good and wonderful things.

120. **Communication** – "I love you," meaning I communicate to and with you. I ardently desire to understand exactly what it is you wish to communicate to me and I want you to understand me.

121. **Welcome** – "I love you," meaning I open my arms to you. You are highly invited and warmly welcome into my space and into my place. You are a guest of honor.

122. **Concern** – "I love you," meaning I am concerned for you. I will try not to worry over you, but I am genuinely concerned for your safety and security, your protection and your welfare.

123. **Charity** – "I love you," meaning I give to you in need. Please accept my charitable works, things, or money to help you out in basic ways. I help and give simply because you are in need.

124. **In love** – "I love you," meaning I am in love with you. I am feeling great and wonderful feelings of love. I am greatly attracted to you and you are appealing in many different ways. I am caught up and wrapped up in strong feelings.

125. **Justice** – "I love you," meaning I do justice for you. In the face of injustice, I will act and work to bring about justice for you. We all have a right to justice. It is the good and right thing.

126. **Saying No** – "I love you," meaning I say no to you. I will not simply do what you want me to do or give you what you want. I see clearly that "no" is for your real and actual good.

127. **Agreement** – "I love you," meaning I agree with you. In spite of our differences, and our disagreements, I will make an agreement, acceptable to both of us, to move ahead, to have peace.

128. **Compromise** – "I love you," meaning I compromise with you. I will give up something I want for the sake of an agreement and resolution to a problem, for "our" greater good.

129. **Vulnerable** – "I love you," meaning I am vulnerable before you. I open myself to you for you to see my weaknesses and shortcomings. I allow you to see the real and authentic me.

130. **Unexplainable** – "I love you," meaning I don't know what I mean. All I know is that I can't get you out of my mind and it bothers me, but in a good and pleasant way. We need to talk!

131. **Share** – "I love you," meaning I share with you. I see you in need and so I share some of what I have with you. I share my food, my drink, my material things, and other shareable things.

132. **Please** – "I love you," meaning I please you. I do for you to please you. I do many different things for you, depending on what will please you at any given time and moment.

133. **Praise** – "I love you," meaning I praise you for what you have done. I acknowledge your talents, abilities, virtue, or achievement, and I congratulate you. Well done!

134. **In Return** – "I love you," meaning I return in love to you the love you have given to me. Reciprocation is built into human nature. It is natural to respond in like fashion to things given.

135. **Mercy** – "I love you," meaning I extend mercy to you. In your offence, I extend to you an act that goes beyond fairness and justice. Fairness and justice are human; mercy is divine.

136. **Compassion** – "I love you," meaning I have compassion for you. I feel very deeply for you in a kind, caring and loving way. I see your pain or misfortune and I am moved with feeling.

137. **Will** – "I love you," meaning I submit to your will O God. I freely, willingly and humbly submit my will to your will to be directed in my actions according to your will and desire.

138. **Mission** – "I love you," meaning I give myself to you God for the mission marked out for me in this life. Once committed, I stay the course, acting and living dedicated to the task.

139. **Mentor** – "I love you," meaning I mentor you. I help you to grow and develop to become the beautiful person you are capable of becoming. I clarify, listen, guide, explain, and encourage you.

140. **Save** – "I love you," meaning I save you. I save you from danger. I save you from your enemies. I save you from yourself. I save you from harm and destruction. I help save your soul.

141. **Good** – "I love you," meaning I do good for you. I am thinking of your good and desire the good for you. In many and different ways I do things for you that are truly good for you.

142. **Help** – "I love you," meaning I help you. I extend myself, my time, my energy, my skill, my knowledge, my care, my concern, to help you in your situation in which you need help.

143. **Chastise** – "I love you," meaning I chastise you. I chastise you verbally for your own good. You don't see or don't realize the unhealthy state or condition you are in. You need a jolt.

144. **Humble** – "I love you," meaning I humble myself with you. I humble myself in a healthy way and I make no effort to exercise personal power over you. We are equals as fellow humans.

145. **Counsel** – "I love you," meaning I counsel you. I care deeply for you and I use all my knowledge, skill, and experience of life, to counsel you to help you personally and practically.

146. **Prudence** – "I love you," meaning I do the right thing at the right time for you. I am very conscious of the fact that the good in particular situations often demands thought and effort.

147. **Temperance** – "I love you," meaning I exercise temperance for you. I moderate my feelings, passions, and energies. I exercise self-control for your good.

148. **Gift** – "I love you," meaning I give a gift to you. The gift I give you freely is a sign of my love for you. The gift I give is given with feeling and affection from my heart. Please accept it.

149. **Celebrate** – "I love you," meaning I celebrate you. I join in celebrating some significant thing about you, because you are a significant person and individual worth celebrating!

150. **Perseverance** – "I love you," meaning I persevere for you. I make the effort to remain on task, stay on course, not give up, complete the work, and endure hardship, all for your good.

151. **Enemy** – "I love you," meaning I wish you well, intend and do good for you in spite of our antagonism, differences, and negative feelings towards each other. This is very difficult to do.

152. **Available** – "I love you," meaning I am available for you. I avail myself and give my time to you when you need me. When the need arises, I make time for you, for your good.

153. **Flexible** – "I love you," meaning I am flexible for you. I am willing to change my plans, my schedule, and my flow of activities to accommodate you for your good.

154. **Collaborate** – "I love you," meaning I collaborate with you. I join with you to accomplish some work or project for our collective good or for the common good of others.

155. **Make amends** – "I love you," meaning I make amends for the wrong and offense I have done. I am truly sorry and I wish to make up for it. I will make amends with real action.

156. **Attention** – "I love you," meaning I give you attention. I notice you; I see what you're wearing; I give you time; I respond to you; I ask you how you are. I attend to you.

157. **Life** – "I love you," meaning I give you life. I imagine and dream of you. I intend and will you to exist. I plan for you to be conceived. You exist! You have life! My offspring – my child.

158. **Name** – "I love you," meaning I name you and give you identity. You are "a somebody" with your own name and title. We can all call you by name. Your name is special.

159. **Enlightenment** – "I love you," meaning I enlighten you. I wish to shed light upon your mind, soften the hardness of your heart and lighten up the darkness of your soul.

160. **Invitation** – "I love you," meaning I invite you. I think of you, of your good, and I invite and offer you an opportunity to join in, take part, see, experience, do, if you would like.

161. **Opportunity** – "I love you," meaning I give you an opportunity, for your good. You can grow, develop, and actualize your potential by taking advantage of this opportunity.

162. **Honor** – "I love you," meaning I honor you. I acknowledge and hold you in esteem for the person you are, the good you have done or the accomplishment you have achieved.

163. **Mourn** – "I love you," meaning I mourn with you. I join in sympathy and compassion with you in your loss of a loved one or the loss of something very dear to you. I am with you in spirit.

164. **Peace** – "I love you," meaning I wish peace upon you. I desire, intend and work to bring about inner peace for you amid the strife, confusion, busyness, and stress of life.

165. **Allow to love** – "I love you," meaning I allow you to love. I give you space to think and feel, and simply be and to respond and act with love. I give you freedom to be authentic.

166. **Anticipate** – "I love you," meaning I anticipate your needs and wishes. I think ahead and I am ready to do and to respond positively and effectively for you, for your good.

167. **Silence** – "I love you," meaning I remain silent. I don't need to fill the space between us with noise. You are O.K. You don't have to prove anything. In silence, I sense the love.

168. **No Words** – "I love you," meaning I don't speak. Words are not required or necessary. Look in my eyes. Observe my actions. See how I move. Actions are stronger than words.

169. **Accommodation** – "I love you," meaning I accommodate you. I take into consideration what you need, want and desire and I change, adjust, alter my actions and plans for your good.

170. **Lose** – "I love you," meaning I lose the "game" on purpose for you. I don't tell you or make it obvious, but the outcome of the game or competition is secondary. You are primary.

171. **Virtue** – "I love you," meaning I develop inner virtue within myself to love you greater, higher, and deeper. The virtues motivate and enable me to love you more and more.

172. **Command** – "I love you," meaning I command you, while respecting your freedom and dignity. A command is necessary, good, and just. What I say is clearly for your good.

173. **Little acts of love** – "I love you," meaning "may every beat of my heart, every blink of my eyes, every step I take and every breath of air I breathe in, be an act of love for you, my God."

174. **Accountability** – "I love you," meaning I am calling you to account for what you said or did. It needs to be addressed and dealt with. You need to change or stop the action, for your own good.

175. **Real** – "I love you," meaning I desire to be real to you and I desire to see and know the real you. Reality and truth are important to me, to you, to us. The real is good, true, and beautiful.

176. **Spousal Commitment** – "I love you," meaning I commit to you in marriage. I pledge myself to you alone and I commit and give myself to you like no other. You are special to me.

177. **Erotic** – "I love you," meaning I am aroused sensually and sexually by you, by your physical anatomy and appearance. I want to channel this energy for your good and for our wholesome and moral good.

178. **Emotive** – "I love you," meaning I value all the emotions I have for you. I enjoy all the good, positive feelings I have and that we share together. I possess feelings of love for you.

179. **Withhold** – "I love you," meaning I withhold something from you for your good. I don't give you something you want. I don't tell you about things you should not hear and know about.

180. **Considerate** – "I love you," meaning I am considerate of you. I am attuned to your concerns, needs, wants, desires, problems, and difficulties. I consider what you say and don't say.

181. **Worry** – "I love you," meaning I am concerned for your well-being. My concern and worry is natural because I desire what is good and best for you.

182. **Boundaries** – "I love you," meaning I set boundaries for us. The boundaries I set for the two of us in this particular relationship are good and healthy for you and for me.

183. **Take seriously** – "I love you," meaning I take you seriously. What you say and do, what you think and feel, what you believe and hold, are all important to me. You are important to me.

184. **Hope** – "I love you," meaning I have hope in you. I hold and believe in good things for you and for the future. I keep positive and hopeful for your happiness and well-being.

185. **Precious** – "I love you," meaning you are precious to me. Words of love are one way to express the reality of your uniqueness, and being special and precious to me.

186. **Transformation** – "I love you," meaning I will help in a personal transformation. With you open and willing, I can help you change and transform yourself as a person and human being.

187. **Speechless** – "I love you," meaning there is no word to adequately name and no words to accurately describe and explain the love I have for you. The reality is beyond words.

188. **Open and Willing** – "I love you," meaning I am open to truth, to God, to good, to others, and to you. I am open to do what is right and to do what is good. I am willing to change.

189. **Alive** – "I love you," meaning I have come alive because of you. I feel alive with you. I feel good and great, optimistic and full of energy! I am happy and I want to be with you.

190. **Wake up!** – "I love you," meaning I want to wake you up. I want you to realize the dangers you are putting yourself in or the unhealthy situation you are in. Change before it's too late.

191. **Appreciation** – "I love you," meaning I really value and treasure what you have done for me. I am deeply moved and I appreciate your action. Your thought and effort mean a lot to me.

192. **Gratitude** – "I love you," meaning I truly and deeply thank you. I am so very grateful for what you have given me - your self, your time, your gift, your help, and your things. Thank you!

193. **Fear** – "I love you," meaning I fear to cause ill or negativity to you. I am afraid to offend you. I am afraid to cause you pain. I am afraid to injure or jeopardize our relationship.

194. **Seeking the Lost** – "I love you," meaning I know you are lost either physically or in other ways, and I am looking for you, seeking you out, so that I can truly and sincerely help you.

195. **Hear Your Cry** – "I love you," meaning I sense your silent cry for help; I read between the lines your needing help. I hear your words, "please help me," and I gladly and willingly respond.

196. **Food** – "I love you," meaning I feed you food and nourish your physical body. I satisfy your appetite and hunger. I attend to one of your basic needs and I want to make you happy.

197. **Family** – "I love you," meaning I create a family for you, for your growth and development, for your sense of security and need for belonging, for your well-being and good.

198. **Fun** – "I love you," meaning I provide fun for you, for your enjoyment and happiness. I have fun with you and share it with you. Fun is a natural thing and I see the need and place for it.

199. **Occupation** – "I love you," meaning I do my very best in my occupation to serve you and others for your good and well-being. Doing my job well has an effect on others for their benefit.

200. **Vocation** – "I love you," meaning I am faithful to my calling in life and I carry it out to the best of my abilities for your good and the good of others. I take my vocation and you seriously.

201. **Proud** – "I love you," meaning I am so very proud of you. I am full of healthy pride in you for being a fine and good person. I am proud of your accomplishments and achievements.

202. **Check** – "I love you," meaning I am just checking to see if everything is all right. I just want to confirm the time, location, and the details to ensure a good and positive outcome. I just want to make sure that you are safe.

203. **Fortitude** – "I love you," meaning I muster up my inner strength for you, for your good. I develop inner strength to overcome hardships and difficulties for your benefit.

204. **Labor of love** – "I love you," meaning I devote myself to this labor of love for your good. I persevere and bring it to completion in anticipation of the positive results it will bring.

Negative and Unhealthy Faces
of Love

1. **Obsession** – "I love you," meaning I am obsessed with you. I have an unhealthy and uncontrollable attraction, desire, and need for you. My behavior is irrational and unpredictable.

2. **Sex** – "I love you," meaning I only want to have sex with you. I want pleasure and the experience of the physical act of sexual intercourse. I am only thinking of myself. You are an object to me.

3. **Rebound** – "I love you," meaning I need you to fill me. I need you to fill the emptiness and void, to soothe the hurt, and alleviate the pain. I need you to replace the person I no longer have.

4. **Enmeshment** – "I love you," meaning I am enmeshed with you. We are enmeshed with each other. We are bound and tied to each other negatively. We are in a dysfunctional relationship.

5. **Narcissism** – "I love you," meaning I love myself. In all my words and actions, I really am wanting something for me, for my good or benefit, for whatever suits me. I am wholly selfish.

6. **Pseudo / False** – "I love you," meaning I say I love you, but my deeds and actions are not good, positive or healthy for you. This is a faulty understanding and perception of real love.

7. **Before I Knew You** – "I love you," meaning I imagined a person and love like you. Before I saw or knew anything about you, I loved you. I do not love the real person but an ideal.

8. **Self-destructive** – "I love you," meaning I am dying in my love for you. My love for you is having a negative effect on me. It is not healthy or life-giving. It is objectively flawed somehow.

9. **Seduction** – "I love you," meaning I seduce you. I knowingly misinform and mislead you to get what I want from you. I deceive you to get what I want, whether it is sexual or otherwise.

10. **Desperation** – "I love you," meaning I am desperate for you. I have to have you. I need to have you. I need you to love me. I don't know what I'll do without you. I'm completely lost without you.

11. **Fatal Attraction** – "I love you," meaning I am extremely attracted to you, but not for my good. I am very attracted to you but our relationship is going to be negative, unhealthy, and bad.

12. **Blind** – "I love you," meaning I see you as perfect. You have no faults and everything you do and everything about you is wonderful. I only see your good qualities. I don't see the real you.

13. **Reckless Abandon** – "I love you," meaning I abandon my mind and let my emotions and passions dictate my action. It may feel liberating but the flight from reality will eventually crash.

14. **Idol** – "I love you," meaning I idolize you. You are my perfect hero or heroine and the absolute greatest. You are above all else. Behavior borders on worship. This is extreme and disordered for God alone is meant to be our idol.

15. **Die** – "I love you," meaning I give up my life and I would rather die if I can't be with you. I love you so much and I can't bear to live without you. This is not love. It is capitulation and a warped sense of love.

16. **Co-dependency** – "I love you," meaning we are highly dependent upon each other in a negative and unhealthy way. We feed off and reinforce each other's weaknesses and deficiencies.

17. **Lust** – "I love you," meaning I lust after you. My senses and imagination focus on your body and sex. I derive sensory pleasure from this. I see you as an object and not as a person.

18. **Affair** – "I love you," meaning I am involved with you emotionally and sexually within a marriage relationship. This is a grave violation of the marriage bond, trust, and commitment.

19. **Manipulation** – "I love you," meaning I manipulate you. I use these emotionally charged words to cause you to let your guard down and then manipulate you for my selfish intentions.

20. **Imposition** – "I love you," meaning I impose what I want on you. I don't ask you or respect you. I impose my thoughts, my will, my wants, my desires, my actions, and my intentions upon you.

21. **Lie** – "I love you," meaning I deliberately lie for you. I don't tell the truth, thinking I can bring about some good for you. Objectively, this is not love but a twisted sense of doing good.

22. **Abuse** – "I love you," meaning I say things to you and do things to you, telling you they are for your good. But actually and objectively, they constitute a form of abuse. They are not good.

23. **Self-indulged** – "I love you," meaning I indulge you in everything you want so you can be happy and comfortable. I am actually spoiling you and forming you in a negative and unhealthy way.

24. **Punch Drunk** – "I love you," meaning I am in a giddy state over you. My head seems to be light and spinning. I don't have a care in the world. This is emotional inebriation, not love.

25. **Enabling** – "I love you," meaning I help you too much and do too much for you, wanting to please you and make you happy. I am actually fostering unhealthy dependence and stifling your growth.

26. **Beat** – "I love you," meaning I physically beat you for your own good, to teach you a lesson or to make sure you don't repeat an undesired action. This is a form of abuse not love.

27. **Submission** – "I love you," meaning I completely submit myself to you. I will do anything you want me to do without question. In human relationships, this is both unhealthy and abnormal.

"The stories of each of our lives, who we are and the character and person we have become, for better or for worse, are really stories about love."

~ Author

St. Paul on Love

I may be able to speak the languages of human beings and even of angels, but if I have no love, my speech is no more than a noisy gong or a clanging bell. I may have the gift of inspired preaching; I may have all knowledge and understand all secrets; I may have all the faith needed to move mountains – but if I have no love, I am nothing. I may give away everything I have, and even give up my body to be burned – but if I have no love, this does me no good.

Love is patient and kind; it is not jealous or conceited or proud; love is not ill-mannered or selfish or irritable; love does not keep a record of wrongs; love is not happy with evil, but is happy with the truth. Love never gives up; and its faith, hope, and patience never fail.

Love is eternal. There are inspired messages, but they are temporary; there are gifts of speaking in strange tongues, but they will cease; there is knowledge, but it will pass. For our gifts of knowledge and of inspired messages are only partial; but when what is perfect comes, then what is partial will disappear.

When I was a child, my speech, feelings, and thinking were all those of a child; now that I am an adult, I have no more use for childish ways. What we see now is like a dim image in a mirror; then we shall see face-to-face. What I know now is only partial; then it will be complete – as complete as God's knowledge of me.

Meanwhile these three remain: faith, hope, and love; and the greatest of these is love.

1 Corinthians 13

Conclusion

This book, despite its title and fundamental theme and message of believing, is actually a book about truth. Belief and believing were never meant to be terminal points and ends in themselves. Believing was not primarily intended for us to feel good or derive comfort and security from the act, no matter how strong or devoted a believer we may be. To focus on belief as deriving personal significance and meaning for oneself only is really to stay within the realm of self. To remain within the realm of subjective experience is to remain forever burdened and shackled with the chains of subjectivity, where there is no objective truth, but only an individual's own thoughts, ideas, perceptions, opinions, experiences, and meaning. In the moral sphere, the individual is doomed to moral relativism, intoxicating for a time, but deadly in its inevitable and painful crash to hard reality. Serious intellectual skepticism and entrenched moral relativism will always lead to a lonely and miserable existence and life, empty and joyless, devoid of the truth and good that ultimately satisfies and fulfills the yearning of the human spirit.

All humans were made to know the truth of things and the human intellect can attain objective truth. We do this by going beyond ourselves, by transcending the physical and our very selves, and making a real connection with that which is real. We have the capacity to transcend the veil of the physical and personal subjectivity and begin to see the beautiful truths contained in beliefs, ideals, values, principles, and practices. The act of believing and the beliefs we hold are meant to be "stepping stones" to truth. They are the simple, common, and practical ways by which we can attain the truth of life, living, ourselves, the world, God, and many other known realities of existence. Thus, believing is good and essential for all humans, not just Christians, in so far as believing leads and directs us to truth and what can be known as true in this life.

The first question of truth is, "What is truth?" Over two thousand years ago, Pilate asked Jesus this same question. Jesus was silent and did not answer. I believe Jesus was silent for two reasons. The answer to the question is self-evident to the sincere and intellectually humble person, and either you see it or you don't. It is like asking a person if they exist. You cannot prove or convince someone of something that is self-evident by something that is less evident. Jesus chose not to engage with Pilate in his question, perhaps knowing that it would be a futile effort and waste of time. The common sense answer which any normal person realizes with minimal thought is that *truth is the correspondence of the intellect to reality.* If what is in the mind corresponds to what is really there outside the mind, you have truth. I believe the main reason why Jesus was silent was because Pilate was actually in the presence of Truth. He couldn't have been any closer. Pilate was looking at Truth directly in the eyes and he did not see or acknowledge Jesus as such. Jesus is the Way, the Truth, and the Life; Jesus is the full embodiment of truth and *is* Truth. Jesus Himself was *the* answer to Pilate's question, but Jesus knew there was nothing He could say that would prove or convince Pilate of it.

The silence of Jesus perhaps points to another truth, namely that the nature of truth is such that it finds its place and rest in the intellect only if it is desired and welcomed. The imprint of truth upon the mind usually happens slowly and gently, gaining strength and authority by it own accord and character. Jesus was heard telling his followers not to cast pearls before the swine. He Himself followed His own teaching by not openly speaking and revealing the truth before someone who didn't sincerely desire it and wasn't open to know and accept the truth in the first place.

The second question of truth is, "Can we know truth? Can we know something as objectively true?" People acknowledge that we can indeed know the truth of things, but we are limited to only those things within the realm of our own direct experience. In this manner of thinking, all statements, propositions, values and principles of a universal nature are relegated to individual opinion and personal belief. On the contrary, I boldly assert that you and I and all human beings can certainly attain and possess truth outside of our so called "own direct experience." We do this by transcending the material and physical, which confines us to time and place and peer into the realm of the real, universal, objective, and true. We attain truth by transcending our egos and subjective perceptions and experiences. We are spiritual and transcendent beings, with immortal souls with the immaterial powers of intellect and will. We are able to reason, judge, choose and love. Knowing and loving are the two fundamental human activities that allow us to transcend ourselves. When we attain, know, and possess the truth, we go beyond our particular individual selves to the universal and objective true and good of reality. When we truly love, we go beyond our particular individual selves to the personal and objective true and good of the other. Yes, we can know truth! Our mind was made for truth and it will only be satisfied when in the possession of truth. God is a transcendent

Being. Only in knowing and loving God do we truly connect, experience, and have a relationship with God. This is why many people do not sense and feel the real presence of God.

The third question of truth is, "How can I attain truth?" We can attain and come to knowledge of truth in several basic and varied ways. I refer to them as *pathways of certitude*, which refer to the different paths we can take in order to attain truth. Like traveling to a destination, there are different roads and possible routes to get us there. The journey is one thing; arriving at your destination is another. The certitudes are like the roads and the journey, whereas truth is likened to arriving at your destination and goal. Often we take several different roads along the overall route of our trip; likewise, we often combine several different certitudes in our overall search and attainment of the truth. I propose and outline the following *pathways of certitude*, which are possible ways of attaining truth:

Experiential certitude – We can know as true those things that are within the realm of our direct experience. We know what our senses tell us – what we see, hear, taste, smell, and touch. We know our own internal activities and our reactions to things around us. "I know the apple is red. I know I am not comfortable with how that person spoke to me. I know I am nervous about the interview. I know the music is too loud for me. I know I am hungry." This basic certitude covers a very broad range, but nevertheless it is limited.

Certitude of judgment – We can know as true those things that are self-evident. Judgment is one of the powers of the intellect and as such, when functioning correctly, judges simply and correctly. We don't require a reasoning process but a simple judgment based upon experience and common sense. "I know things are what they are. This is the principle of identity. I know something cannot be and not be at the same time in the same respect. This is the principle of non-contradiction. I know human freedom is a power that I exercise. I know there is a real world outside of my mind and direct experience. I know a self-evident moral first principle is do good and avoid evil."

Moral certitude – We can know as true those things that we have no reason to doubt their veracity. We are told things; we hear things; we read things. There is human consensus that a statement or proposition is true. There is no good reason to doubt it and therefore it is reasonable accept the truth of the statement. "I know the earth and other planets revolve around the sun. although I have never witnessed the fact. I know Moscow, Nairobi, and Rio de Janeiro are actual cities, although I have never been to those places. I know Neil Armstrong set foot on the moon, although I was not there when it happened. I know my mother and father are my biological parents, although I have no recollection of my birth and the first years of my life."

Historical certitude – We can know as true those things that are reported to us accurately and correctly by scholars and researchers. We believe in the word of authoritative and credible historians. There is human and academic consensus concerning the people and events of the past. "I know Thomas Jefferson drafted the Declaration of Independence in 1776. I know Johannes Gutenberg invented the printing press around 1450. I know a man named Jesus from the city of Nazareth claimed to be God and was crucified and died on a cross, about 2000 years ago. I know Thales, Socrates, Plato, and

Aristotle were Greek thinkers and philosophers who lived before the common era."

Predictable certitude – We can know as true those things that have been happening the same way constantly and continuously, and there is nothing to indicate there will be a change. We can accurately and correctly predict outcomes and draw conclusions. "I know the sun will rise tomorrow morning. I know there will be snow this winter where I live. I know the population of the world increases every year. I know school is a place where I can get an education. I know I will not live on this earth forever."

Scientific certitude – We can know as true those things that the scientific community discovers to be factual. Through hypothesis, observation, experimentation, measuring, weighing, testing, and concluding, we can know the truth about the physical world. Science reasons to general principles, theories, theorems, and conclusions. "I know all physical elements are either a solid, liquid, or gas. I know food contains nutrition, required to fuel the body and keep it alive and functioning. I know rocket fuel is highly combustible and has great explosive power. I know water is composed of two hydrogen atoms and one oxygen atom."

Certitude of belief – We can know as true those things that others say, by trusting them and believing what they tell us. The witnesses must be not be lying or deceiving us, nor must they be deceived themselves. What they tell us must be true and in believing them as a credible witness, we come to knowledge of the truth. "I know the Knights won the football game because coach Smith told me. I know I was born at the

Edmonton General because my parents told me. I know the price of housing in Switzerland is relatively expensive because my sister who lives there told me. I know my brother moved into his new house because he told me. I know my daughter is enjoying her year at university because she told me."

Certitude of faith – We can know as true those things that God reveals to us and tells us. God is Truth and whatever God says is true. God does not deceive nor can He be deceived. By believing what God says, we possess the truth. It's as simple as that. "I know God is a personal intelligence because He reveals His intelligence by His intricate design and order in the universe. I know I am called to love God and my neighbor because Jesus directed us to do so. I know heaven exists because Jesus spoke of paradise. I know the Beatitudes are important for living because Jesus taught them to his followers. I know Jesus will be with us always because he said so, "And I will be with you always, to the end of the age."

Certitude of illumination – We can know as true those things that we receive through the inspiration, enlightenment, and illumination of the Holy Spirit. "Then He opened their minds to understand the Scriptures…" The Holy Spirit is the Spirit of love and of truth, empowering us to love, and also enabling us to see and know the truth, especially pertaining to spiritual things and things of God. The Holy Spirit sheds light upon our minds, whether it is candle light, a hundred watt bulb, or a tremendous flash of blinding light like was given to St. Paul. One reflects upon their own internal activities and senses that there is another mind, voice and spirit present. This is the Spirit of God. "I know there is right and wrong because my conscience, the voice of God within me, tells me so. I know we are called to love and personal holiness because God reminds me internally and quietly." Mother Teresa acknowledged publicly that it was the Spirit of God within her that enabled and empowered her to have the motivation and strength to serve the world's poorest of the poor daily. The Gospel writers were inspired by the Holy Spirit to write in words the messages and truths God wanted to communicate.

Logical certitude – We can know as true those things that we arrive at through formal logic and the power of reasoning. A conclusion is drawn, which was not apparent at the onset, through a thought and reasoning process. We have premises and a conclusion. Two true premises plus correct reasoning yields a true conclusion. For example, a = b, and b = c, therefore a = c. In deduction, we reason from the general to the particular. "I know all saintly persons love God. I know Susan is a saintly person. Therefore, I know Susan loves God." With induction, if every case and instance of x that we observe and study equals y, we conclude that all x equals y. For example, x1 = y, x2 = y, x3 =y, x4 = y, x5 = y, therefore x = y. We reason from the particular to the general. "I observe (know) that particular humans Joachim, Elsie, Chiaki, Ise, Bill, Doris, Regina, Peter, Mike, Angie, Dominik, Pauline, Dave, Tom, Mary Anne, Theresa, Michael, Marianne, Anthony, Paul, Petey, Christina, Alex, Charlotte, Rebecca, Julia, William, Joey, Luke, Mickey, David, Frances, Angela, Daniel, Laura, Chris, Adam, and Naomi need food, drink, rest and sleep. Therefore I conclude (know) that human beings need food, drink, rest and sleep." We can attain the truth of things in so far as the premises and observations we begin with are accurate and true, and our reasoning process is correct and faultless.

The ten *pathways of certitude* are ten possible ways that we as human beings can attain truth. This is not to say that everybody takes advantage of these pathways, and that all people travel at the same speed or in the same fashion. I am not saying that we will always attain truth along each of the pathways with every instance or attempt. In each of the ten pathways to truth, there are certain conditions which must necessarily be met. If my senses (i.e. eyesight) are faulty, I may be mistaken in what I see and hence not attain the truth. If I make a faulty judgment, I put myself in error, not in the possession of truth. If the consensus of society is wrong then I am in the possession of a falsehood, not a truth. If the historian has made an error in calculation or translation, then the error is passed on to me. If there is a freak occurrence in nature, my expectation of what should happen will not happen. If the conclusion of a scientific theory is actually false, then I will not have a true conclusion. If someone tells me a lie, then I will adopt a lie, not a truth. If I didn't correctly get what God revealed, then what I believe will not be correct, despite my sincere act of believing. If I don't have an accurate understanding of what Jesus means by the words He said, then what I believe will not be accurate. If the spirit which I believe enlightens me is not of God, then the truth of the perceived illumination is entirely called into question. If the premises which I begin with are not true, then my logical conclusions will not be true. If my premises and observations are true, but my reasoning is faulty, then my conclusions will not be correct. Truth implies correspondence and it must necessarily be present for truth to exist in the mind. Otherwise, we fall short. Whenever we do not achieve correspondence and truth, the shortcoming is always on the side of the human mind, not objective reality.

The substance of life is not the climbing a ladder of absolute certainties but rather swimming in the murky, uncertain, and sometimes treacherous waters of living. Although we can attain absolute certainties with some things and there are absolutes, the common experience of humankind is that those things are the exception and not the rule. God is absolute Truth and happy and blessed are those who see this. We can know with absolute certainty that God exists. Exactly what God says and what it means is another thing and it is not always clear and absolute. I assert that we are able to ascertain truth concerning what God says and means but we must not be hasty. Rather we must always allow the Spirit of Truth to guide and direct us to the truth. We must be very careful when it comes to making absolute claims and statements, especially when actions and practical consequences closely follow. Many horrendous acts throughout history have been perpetrated in the name of God. Indifference, hatred, fighting, killing, and wars have been justified by man in the name of God. Yes, we must literally fight evil but we must do it according to God's ways. Yes, we must defend against the unjust aggressor but never be the offensive aggressor ourselves. Yes, we are called to combat lies and falsehoods and be a witness to the truth, but we must do it without resorting to violence. The fact remains that we must separate that which is of God and that which is of human sin and ignorance. Granted, this is not always easy. We are helped when we remember the universal truth of human experience that reminds us, "By their fruits you shall know them." The Fruits of the Spirit are love, joy, peace, patience, kindness, goodness, faithfulness, gentleness, and self-control. Judge for yourself. Be careful when you hear claims of absolute certainty, knowing that with humans there can be absolute self-deception, both individually and collectively.

There are times when we are mistaken, deceived, wrong, in error, and simply do not possess the truth. This should not surprise us because we are imperfect beings and imperfections in our knowing and doing are both natural and inevitable. The fact that we are sinful at times should not erase the merits of our virtue or downgrade the fact that we are good and loving as well. The fact that we are ignorant and make intellectual errors at times should not erase the value of our knowledge or downgrade the fact that we have truth and wisdom also. Life is an art, not a science. The domain of truth is life, more so a life lived fully and lived well, not the university laboratory or an ivory tower of learning. Truth is the common commodity of every human being, not just for the learned few.

There can be many obstacles and doubts placed in front of us, to hinder us from attaining and possessing truth. Truth loves to hide and so we have to work for it, if we want to savor its taste and enjoy its benefits. I liken the attainment of truth to scoring a touchdown after a grueling ninety-yard run, evading crushing tackles and menacing opposition, never giving up until the pigskin crosses the goal line. "Hurray – Touchdown! Hurray – Truth!" I picture the hockey player gather the puck behind his net, stick handle through the entire opposing team, face the masked goaltender, fake a shot and raise the puck high over the outstretched net minder. "Wow – I score! Wow – I see the truth!" I envision the mountain climber in her conquest of Mount Everest, after several base camps, weeks of acclimatization, days of dangerous climbing, reaching the summit and planting her flag at the top of the world. "Thank God – I made it! Thank you God – I have the truth!" Yes, truth is both possible and attainable. Many others have said it before – "Those who sincerely seek the truth will find it."

Finally, all the questions of life and living that can and ever will be asked, are really questions of truth and love, and all the answers are ultimately answered in and of God. Believing leads to knowing, knowing to loving, and loving to God. Faith leads to truth, truth to love, and all three lead to God!

Epilogue

"Life is a personal challenge and one long journey, but we do not struggle and travel alone. Life is a big adventure and a unique odyssey but we do not venture and wander by ourselves. Life is an individual and personal endeavor and also a family, community, and global project. The truth of life is that we are all in this together. We all inherit the two-fold darkness of sin and ignorance into which we are born and live. To some degree, we're all selfish and do stupid things. We all feel the cutting edge of indifference, greed, and injustice and experience pain, suffering, and the hardships of life. With love in our hearts, truth in our minds, goodness in our wills, hope in our spirits, faith in our souls, and God in everything, the challenges of our lives will prove to be manageable – yes, but more than that, they may be wonderful, and perhaps even joyful. Believe."

~ Michael Joachim Girard

Printed in the United States
55790LVS00007B/43-75